ANCIENT WISDOM, MODERN SCIENCE

Ancient Wisdom,
MODERN SCIENCE

The Integration of Native Knowledge in Math and Science at Tribally Controlled Colleges and Universities

Edited by Paul Boyer

Published by Salish Kootenai College Press, Pablo, Montana
Distributed by University of Nebraska Press, Lincoln, Nebraska

Published by Salish Kootenai College Press
PO Box 70
Pablo, MT 59855

Distributed by University of Nebraska Press
1111 Lincoln Mall
Lincoln, NE 68588-0630
order 1-800-755-1105
www.nebraskapress.unl.edu.

ISBN: 978-1-934594-07-0

Library of Congress Cataloging-in-Publication Data

Ancient wisdom, modern science : the integration of Native knowledge in math and science at tribally controlled colleges and universities / edited by Paul Boyer.
    p. cm.
Includes bibliographical references.
ISBN 978-1-934594-07-0
1. Indian universities and colleges—United States. 2. Mathematics—Study and teaching (Higher) 3. Science—Study and teaching (Higher) 4. Indians of North America—Intellectual life. 5. Wisdom. 6. Learning and scholarship—United States. 7. Indians of North America—Education. 8. Multicultural education—United States. I. Boyer, Paul, 1964-
E97.55.A53 2010
970.004'97—dc22
                        2010028117

Cover and text design by Paula Elmes, ImageCraft Publications & Design

Printed in the United States

Contents

Introduction: A New Vision for Math and Science

Paul Boyer

Tribally controlled colleges are institutions of higher learning chartered by one or more Indian tribes and, in most cases, located on Indian reservations. Today, more than thirty-five such institutions are located in fourteen states across the southwest, west, northern Plains and Great Lakes region. Collectively, tribal colleges enroll approximately 30,000 students.

The oldest tribal colleges were established in the late 1960s and early 1970s. They were based on the community college model and, like their mainstream counterparts, emphasized training for local employment. Graduates were prepared for work in fields ranging from construction and welding to secretarial science and vocational nursing. They also provided a general education curriculum for students hoping to transfer to four-year colleges. In these ways, tribal colleges looked and acted like any other community college, their small size and obvious poverty notwithstanding.

Unlike mainstream colleges, however, tribal colleges also attempted to reflect and promote the culture of their communities. Even in their first years, most offered courses in the history, language, philosophy and arts of their tribe. After decades of forced assimilation, they hoped to sustain and, when necessary, rebuild the traditional knowledge of their elders. This combination of vocational education and cultural renewal was typically described at the "dual mission" of the tribal college movement.

Tribal colleges embraced their cultural role and even in their earliest years most offered courses that helped sustain the unique knowledge of their communities. Navajo Community College taught rug weaving, for example, while Lummi Indian College (now Northwest Indian College) offered a course in totem pole carving and Salish Kootenai College in western Montana taught a course in traditional storytelling. It was possible to study the Crow language at Little Big Horn College and Lakota philosophy at Sinte Gleska College (now Sinte Gleska University).

But even in their early years, some tribal college leaders were trying to do even more. It was not enough to teach *about* Native culture; any college could do that. Instead, they were looking for ways to integrate traditional knowledge throughout the entire curriculum. Just as mainstream colleges naturally reflect the values and expectations of Western society in their work, tribal colleges were attempting to integrate Native knowledge and values into the full scope of their programs. The goal was to teach every course from a Native perspective and with Native knowledge.

This attempt to "Indianize" the curriculum was most easily accomplished in the humanities and social sciences. It is relatively easy to introduce a tribal perspective in history, philosophy, psychology, political science and related disciplines. Creative instructors devised their own reading lists and invited tribal elders into the classroom, bringing a fresh perspective to these academic subjects.

But other disciplines were more resistant to change—especially math and the hard sciences. Many instructors wanted to fulfill their college's cultural mandate, but didn't know how to incorporate culture into what seemed to be inherently "non-Indian" disciplines. Twenty years ago former Turtle Mountain College President Carty Monette admitted that while the integration of culture in math and science was a priority for the college, it was "easier said than done."

Still, a great deal of experimentation was taking place. During my visits to tribal colleges in the mid 1980s, I noted that one college had painted a giant mural of the Aztec calendar on a classroom wall. The president told me that students began their math course by investigating the contributions of Aztec scholars before turning their attention to a conventional course of study. This reminded students that math was part of their Native heritage. At Turtle Mountain College, meanwhile, I toured a class taught by an energetic math instructor who was trying to make her subject more accessible by encouraging students to work together to solve problems. She felt that Indian students preferred cooperation over competition.

At the time, all this was cutting edge and there was an air of excitement about the work, especially when it seemed to increase student academic success. Looking back, however, it's clear that there was also a pronounced reluctance to modify the core content of science courses, alter conventional pedagogy, or rethink the larger role of math and science in the curriculum. Small cultural elements could be introduced, but the core elements of Western math and science instruction remained largely untouched.

Until now. Over the past decade and, especially, within the last several years, a new vision for math and science education has taken root. Inspired by the writings of the late Vine Deloria and other Indian scholars, tribal college faculty and key administrators are attempting to take control of the science curriculum and create courses and whole degree programs that link Native and Western ways of knowing. With growing confidence, colleges are validating traditional tribal knowledge and exploring scientific concepts from a Native perspective.

Signs of innovation are everywhere. Several tribal colleges are creating courses in ethnobotany, which incorporate Native knowledge into biology and environmental science. Others are investigating archeoastronomy, which draws on traditional star knowledge. A growing number of colleges are also creating new interdisciplinary degree programs that link engineering programs with a larger vision for environmental stewardship and economic sustainability. And many are taking an active part in the national movement promoting undergraduate student research. Every semester, dozens of tribal college students can be found in the field, investigating the environmental and cultural concerns of their reservation communities.

At this exciting moment in the tribal college movement, seven tribal college faculty and administrators from a diverse range of institutions were invited to describe how they are working in practical ways to develop courses, degree programs, and research projects in math and science that also strengthen their college's cultural mission. The following chapters don't encompass all the changes taking place, but they do illustrate the diversity and creativity of math and science education as we enter the second decade of the twenty-first century.

There is great diversity among the courses and programs described here. However, all embrace the intellectual integrity of Native knowledge. Many of the authors forcefully reject the long-held assumption that traditional Native knowledge is outdated and irrelevant to modern society. Instead, they are guided by the belief that the traditional wisdom of Native communities represents a legitimate form of scholarship that is different from, but not inferior to, Western conceptions of science. As Michael Wasseigig Price observes, "This evolution of indigenous knowledge recognizes that our ancestors possessed their own intricate understanding of natural processes and the landscape which allowed them to co-habitate and survive on the earth for millennia." He notes that Native knowledge, based on centuries of observation, can be both richer and deeper than Western science, which is young and incomplete.

Embedded in this movement is a deep respect for local expertise. Instructors are learning to draw on the knowledge of elders and some are taking their courses out of the classroom altogether, relying instead on experiential learning and field observation. Looking for knowledge from within the community, asserts Sharon Kinley, Northwest Indian College's Director of the Coast Salish Institute, is an act of "decolonization." By drawing on tribal knowledge, she says, the college is "helping students relearn their personal and community history. We are helping them regain their connections to the land."

It is important to stress that this philosophy of education is not anti-Western, anti-science or anti-technology. While some tribal college educators do see Western notions of science as narrow and reductionist, most don't pit one form of knowledge against the other. Instead, the two ways of knowing are more typically viewed as complementary. The goal is to combine both worldviews, in the right proportions, in order to create something that is both academically rigorous and relevant to the needs of contemporary tribal societies.

Indeed, several of the following chapters illustrate how technology and the scientific method can be seamlessly integrated into a college's cultural mission. At Sitting Bull College, for example, instructor Jeremy Guinn describes how students are using skills learned in the science lab to monitor water quality and pollution levels on the Standing Rock Reservation. Through science, tribal members are able to take responsibility for the care of their Native lands. And Navajo Technical College is engaged in an ambitious program to bring wireless Internet to the entire Navajo Nation, a region poorly served by existing phone and television service. No longer dependent on outside media, the tribe will be able to offer a range of educational programs developed by and for tribal members.

Math is, in some ways, the problem child of the tribal college curriculum—unloved by students and stubbornly resistant to cultural adaptation. Even here, however, instructors are finding ways to help students see the relevance of the discipline in the larger movement for tribal self determination. At Haskell Indian Nations University, instructor Carol Bowen draws on years of experience and experimentation to help students overcome math anxiety and, above all, see its value in daily life. "Mathematics is strength," she asserts. "Tribes need math to determine and manage budgets, interpret reports, author reports, make policy decisions, manage resources, assess environmental quality, even to determine allotments." Her chapter provides dozens of practical, real world strategies that make math interesting, accessible and relevant.

Collectively, these and other efforts suggest that the larger role of math and science is to support the ongoing effort to strengthen tribes as sovereign nations. In some cases, sovereignty is advanced when tribal members reclaim and embrace their ancestral scholarship; in other cases, sovereignty is advanced when tribes use Western science for their own purposes. In both cases, however, math and science become powerful tools for the advancement of modern tribal cultures.

This book surveys the tremendous progress made and hints at the change to come. Tribal colleges are still young institutions and they continue to grow and change in a variety of ways. In recent decades, they have matured significantly by adding four-year and even graduate programs, building new campus centers, and joining the national network of land grant universities, among other benchmarks of success. Building on this strong foundation, tribal college leaders are demonstrating a willingness to more aggressively assert their identities as Native institutions created for the purpose of strengthening Native nations. We are at the beginning of an exciting new movement.

Paul Boyer authored two reports on the tribal college movement for the Carnegie Foundation for the Advancement of Teaching and is founding editor of the *Tribal College Journal*. Recent publications include *Building Community: Reforming Math and Science Education in Rural Schools* (University of Alaska Press, 2006) and *College Rankings Exposed: The Art of Getting a Quality Education in the 21st Century* (Peterson's, 2003). He holds a doctorate in Educational Theory and Policy from the Pennsylvania State University.

Indigenous Taxonomy, Ethnobotany and Sacred Names

Michael Wassegijig Price

“ Even though the wolverines have long vanished from our forests, if we keep retelling their stories, they may return to us once again. ”

The Ojibwe storyteller, Tobasanokwut from Onigaming First Nations, was referring to the disappearance of the wolverine from the forests of Ontario and how the Anishinaabe oral tradition preserved the stories of this mysterious animal. Wolverines once populated the boreal forests of northern Minnesota, Michigan and southern Ontario. They are solitary scavenging mammals—the largest member of the Weasel family, often possessing a vicious temperament. They are powerful creatures with the jaw strength to tear meat from a frozen carcass. The wolverine is still remembered through the stories and legends of the Anishinaabe people, also known as the Ojibwe or Chippewa people. The Anishinaabe named the wolverine "Gwiingwa'aage—The One Who Came from a Falling Star." The name tells of the wolverine's connection to the star world. After one hundred years of deforestation and fur trapping in North America, the wolverines eventually became extinct from these regions, but their legends are still remembered among tribal peoples.

This chapter is about the integration of Native American language and culture into the science curriculum, and specifically the language and culture of the Anishinaabe people. The Anishinaabe are the people of the Great Lakes region of North America. According to oral tradition, they migrated from the east coast in the regions of Maine and Nova Scotia and eventually settled as far west as Minnesota. Several other bands of Anishinaabe continued to move farther west, including the Turtle Mountain Band of Chippewa of North Dakota, Little Shell Band of Chippewa, and the Rocky Boy Chippewa-Cree in Montana. There are many dialectical differences among the many bands, but they are all considered to be members of the Algonquin language group. Although this chapter is about my personal experience in developing an ethnobotanical curriculum in the Anishinaabe language at Leech Lake Tribal College in Minnesota, this curricular development could apply to any tribal community. This chapter will explore the meaning of indigenous taxonomy and the importance of indigenous languages relative to the study of ecology. I will also discuss my own personal journey in the development of the ethnobotany curriculum within the Anishinaabe language and culture.

Several contemporary terms relating to the integration of indigenous knowledge and science have recently evolved. Native science, traditional ecological knowledge (TEK) and indigenous science are terms that identify this particular evolution of indigenous knowledge relative to what we know as Western science. This evolution of indigenous knowledge recognizes that our ancestors possessed their own intricate understandings of natural processes and landscapes which allowed them to cohabitate and survive on the earth for millennia.

I am beginning to shy away from using the term "science" to describe the nature of indigenous knowledge. Using the label "science" is an invitation for the scientific community to perform dissection and reductionism as methods of validation. I believe that these methods of validation diminish the spiritual connection between knowledge and human beings and therefore cannot be applied to indigenous knowledge. A traditional story or a place name has the power to make us feel connected to that place. The power of a name can change a person's pathway in life or it can change how we interact with or physically respond to a particular entity. Cultural values, as expressed in human attitudes and actions, can affect ecology because people are a part of ecology; indigenous peoples understand this fundamental law. Many contemporary Native thinkers are contemplating how we can safeguard our ancestral knowledge from the reductionist scientific method and articulate a new methodology that fortifies the spirituality of the language and the sacredness of names.

Traditionally, indigenous knowledge was conveyed through storytelling, ceremonies, songs and dances from generation to generation. Today, many of these tribal traditions are slowly disappearing due to globalization and popular culture. However, other forms of cultural conveyance, such as multimedia, cinema, and literature, are being used to pass on the language and culture, which has generated a growing interest among younger generations of Native Americans.

My first major influence in contemplating the link between science and indigenous knowledge was the story told to me of the burning of Manitoulin Island. Like all stories of the indigenous oral tradition, there are several versions depending on the person telling it, but the essence of the story remains the same:

Many years ago, the Anishinaabe lived on a large island among many small islands. There were plenty of berries, deer and fish. The Anishinaabe lived well. Soon, the forests became overgrown; the growth was so thick that the hunters had trouble hunting game. After several years, the berries began to disappear. The forest grew thicker with underbrush. Because there was no more food for them, the rabbits, deer and moose had left the island. Over time, the Anishinaabe grew sick and many began to die of starvation.

A medicine man began to fast to seek a vision for his people. He sat in the forest for four days and nights, and the vision came to him. From that vision, he was told that bad spirits had come to the island and made their home and they had chased away all life. The medicine man instructed all young men to set fire to the forest in the hopes of chasing away the bad spirits. So, the young men went all over the island setting fire to the forests and clearings. The entire island burned. Winter came and the Anishinaabe struggled to survive; many did not live to see the spring.

In the spring, among the ashes and charred trees, small green plants began to emerge like a blanket. The blueberries came back thicker than before. The raspberries returned. Soon the rabbits, moose, and deer returned to the island to graze on the tender grass and shrubs. The hunters could hunt once again. Many berries were dried and stored. The bad spirits that had once settled on the island and chased away life were gone and the Anishinaabe lived well once again.

I was told this story by a respected elder, Honorine Wright, in the summer of 1988 in the town of Wikwemikong on Manitoulin Island, Ontario, Canada—my mother's birthplace. I had just graduated with a bachelor of arts degree in biology from Benedictine College in Atchison, Kansas. With my fresh and unseasoned education in biology, I couldn't help but notice the ecology present in this story. Certainly, the elder telling this story was not educated in the concepts of the biological sciences, yet the story told of forest succession and the ecological relationship between fire and organic life.

Also, in that summer of 1988, during our family visit at Manitoulin Island, an outbreak of wildfires in and around Yellowstone National Park in Wyoming captured the attention of the entire country. June and July were exceptionally dry months, which set the stage for the oncoming fire season. In the eyes of most people, the wildfires were destroying a national treasure and must be subdued at all costs. Firefighters from around the country, including National Guardsmen, were sent out to extinguish the wildfires, but were unsuccessful. Millions of dollars were spent trying to contain one of nature's most ominous forces throughout the hot summer months. It wasn't until late September when the autumn snows began to fall in the mountains that the fires were finally extinguished. Scientists knew that the landscape had been shaped by wildfires for millennia, but the present ideology, which was reflected in the national fire management policies, was that fire must be controlled and suppressed. Smokey the Bear was the symbol of forest fire prevention, a symbol that instilled in generations of children, including Native American children, the notion that wildfires were dangerous.

I soon realized that my indigenous ancestors understood fire and its relationship to the woodland forests, and that their understanding was contained in this story about bad spirits inhabiting the island. It's not surprising that many plains tribes, including the Lakota, Blackfeet and Cheyenne, had periodically set fire to the prairies in order to drive buffalo herds and restore healthy grasslands. It seemed to me as though all indigenous peoples were pyromaniacs! My mind was soon caught up in an ideological whirlwind: Is fire dangerous, or is it healthy for a forest? In thinking about this, the question suddenly occurred to me: What other observations and wisdom are contained within stories, hidden inside the language? Thus began my journey of seeking indigenous knowledge and its connection to ecology.

My career as a tribal college science faculty member began in 1998 at Leech Lake Tribal College located on the reservation of the Leech Lake Band of Ojibwe in northern Minnesota. It was there that I began my investigations into ethnobotany and the Anishinaabe language. I was inspired by the writings of Vine Deloria, Jr. (Standing Rock Lakota), Basil Johnston (Nawash First Nations), Winona LaDuke (White Earth Anishinaabe), Daniel Wildcat (Muscogee) and other Native scholars who were writing about contemporary Native American issues regarding the land. I learned much about the language from Anishinaabe elders like Bob Jourdain, Wallace Humphrey, Tobasanokwut Kinew, and my cousin, Helen Wassegijig. I began harvesting wild rice in the traditional way, learning the Anishinaabe language, and acquainting myself with the native flora of the landscape. My education in biology was beginning to take new form.

What is Indigenous Taxonomy?

Indigenous taxonomy sounds like an oxymoron. Indigenous peoples did not have systematic procedures for naming plants and animals like the binomial nomenclature introduced by Carl Linnaeus in the 1700s, where descriptive Latin names categorically identify individual species by genus and species. However, species were named by indigenous peoples, who sometimes gave several different names for the same species. Though there wasn't a formal method or process of categorization, the names reflect culturally specific understandings of each species. Some names may be thousands of years old while others may have recently evolved, especially with the introduction of exotic plant species. In either case, a specific taxonomy exists within each indigenous culture.

Indigenous languages are a window through which we can see the world from an indigenous perspective. Hidden within the words and phrases of a particular language are observations, relationships, metaphors, and understandings. The Anishinaabe language offers a unique worldview of ecology through the names of plants. Below are three examples of plant names in the Anishinaabe language:

Waaboozojiibik - "Rabbit Root" (waaboozo—rabbit; jiibik—root). This name refers to a particular relationship, currently unknown, between the rabbit and the root of wild sarsaparilla (Aralia nudicaulis).

Ajidamoowano—"Squirrel's Tail" (Ajidamoo—squirrel; wano—tail). This name describes the basal leaves of woolly yarrow (Achillea lanulosa). The leaves have long woolly hairs which resembles a squirrel's bushy tail. The dried flowers of "Ajidamoowano" were smoked ceremonially in stone-carved pipes by the Anishinaabe.

Makizinan—"Moccasins". The word moccasin comes from the Ojibwe word "makizin" referring to a shoe made of buckskin. The Showy Ladyslipper (Cypripedium reginae) is a common orchid that grows in the northern wetlands. The unique shape of its flower inspired the particular style of moccasins that Anishinaabe create.

Indigenous names of plants are descriptive, metaphoric and intertwined with the intricacies of the landscape; they indicate relationships to animals and birds; they describe how the Anishinaabe utilized each plant according to its physical characteristics.

CASE STUDY: WAABIZIIPIN

"White Swan Potatoes" (waabizii—white swan; opin—potato).

THIS IS AN AQUATIC PLANT NAMED "ARROWHEAD" (Sagittaria latifolia) which produces a starchy edible tuber. The tubers grow in the muck just beneath the water. In the autumn, when white swans migrate through the wetland regions of Minnesota, they feed on Waabiziipin. The swans grab hold of the plant and violently flap their wings to pull the tubers from the muck. This harvesting behavior was observed by the Anishinaabe and so named the species.

Anishinaabe women traditionally harvested the tubers in the autumn. Holding onto a canoe, the women would wade out into the marsh and walk around in the muck that contained Waabiziipin plants. The weight of their feet would sever the tubers from the roots and they would eventually float to the surface for gathering. The leaves of Waabiziipin resemble the shape of an arrowhead and are easily identified.

Black ash	*Aagimaak*	"Snowshoe making tree"
Cattails	*Apakweshkwe*	"To place onto the roof"
Fireweed	*Zhooshkojiibik*	"Slippery root"
Goldenrod	*Giiziso mashkikii*	"Sun medicine"
Hepatica	*Animozid*	"Dog tracks"
Pitcher plant	*Omakakiiwidassan*	"Frog leggings"
Poison ivy	*Animikiibag*	"Leaf of the Thunderbirds"
Softstem bulrush	*Anaakanashk*	"Grass for making mats"
Sphagnum moss	*Asaakamig*	"Blanket over the ground"
White ash	*Baapaagimaak*	"Tree of the Woodpeckers"
White water lilly	*Anangobikobiise*	"The star that lives in the water"
Wild rice	*Minoomin*	"The good seed"
Wild strawberry	*Ode'imin*	"The heart fruit"

Different tribal communities within the same region may have different names for a particular species of plant or animal. Unlike the Western paradigms of taxonomic authority, where a distinct genus and species classification becomes universal, there is no conflict over multiple indigenous names for a given species. Tribal communities respect and accept naming differences. The red fox is commonly known among many Anishinaabe communities as "Waagosh" (waa—white; g—connector; osh—tip) referring to the white tip of its fluffy red tail. But on the Red Lake Reservation in northern Minnesota, the red fox is named

CASE STUDY: OMAKAKII

THE COMMON FROG IS NAMED OMAKAKII. Upon learning the Ojibwe language, I began to recognize parts of words connected together. I began to translate the word:

O—pronoun (he/she); *makak*—container; *akii*—earth, ground

The "O" is a pronoun which identifies either "he" or "she". The word "*makak*" is used to describe a container usually made out of birchbark. A simpler translation for *makak* would be "basket". And, finally the word "*akii*" is the word for ground or earth. I postulate that the word "*Omakakii*" translates to "He Who Builds its Lodge in the Earth". This name describes the wintering behavior of the frog which burrows into the soil creating a space for it to hibernate.

"Miskwaje" (miskwaa—red) referring to its bright red fur. The multiple names for the red fox from these different tribal communities add depth and richness to our understanding, and pose no conflict over the validity of its naming. Western scientific circles are not this fluid, and taxonomy therefore becomes a linguistical battleground for recognition and authority.

Common names of cities and states often derive from indigenous place names and the translations of those names tell of a certain characteristic of the landscape:

Michigan	mishigami	"the big lake"
Chicago	Zhigaagong	"where skunks (the pungent ones) live"
Milwaukee	minowaakii	"the good land"
Minnesota	mini shota	"mist over the water" (Dakota)

Bringing Indigenous Names Back to Life

Many Indigenous names of plants, birds and animals are no longer spoken. When the last elder who speaks his or her language fluently dies, that knowledge is lost. Language extinction has already occurred within several tribal communities, such as the Eyak people of Alaska. Those elders who went through the residential school system as children were taught that the indigenous languages are superstitious and backward. They were taught to forget their native tongues because it was shameful. Many elders went to their graves without ever sharing their language or what they learned as children of an indigenous community. This is where language and culture begin to die.

Because of the negative impacts of the federally-sanctioned boarding schools on our parents and grandparents, many cultures became shattered, some more than others. However, many indigenous people of my generation and younger are picking up the pieces of a shattered culture and piecing it back together. The pieces of that culture are the language, place names, medicines, ceremonies and traditions. The pieces of knowledge come from the memory of elders, the craft of storytellers, historical documents, ceremonies and dreams. In those instances, where there are missing pieces, Native people will have to fill those gaps with new ideas, new names and ceremonies. Cultures and languages continue to change throughout time and are never static; they either evolve or devolve.

Indigenous language revitalization efforts are currently underway in both reservation and urban communities. Tribal colleges and tribal schools, in both Canada and the United States, have taken major steps in revitalizing indigenous languages in their communities. The Leech Lake Band of Ojibwe began the Niigaane Ojibwe Language Immersion School for children in preschool through fouth grade. In the Minneapolis-St. Paul area, the Wiconie Nandagikendan Urban Immersion Program delivers Ojibwe and Dakota language immersion education. The Minnesota legislature passed legislation in May 2009 that supports indigenous language revitalization and preservation efforts within tribal communities throughout the state. Minnesota has eleven Native American reservations: four Dakota and seven Ojibwe reservations. The Minnesota Legislature is also discussing possible reforms to the No Child Left Behind Act and its English proficiency testing mandates, which impede elementary-level immersion education programs.

Tribal communities across the country are becoming more proactive in restoring their ancestral languages and cultures by delivering immersion education programs to their children. The Mohawk people in upstate New York formed the Akwesasne Freedom School in 1979 which is centered on Mohawk language and culture, and the Blackfeet people in Montana formed the Piegan Insitute in 1987 in order to rescue their language from extinction. These schools were formed over twenty years ago by tribal activists who saw the need and urgency to revitalize their ancestral language and culture within their communities. Other tribal communities have developed, or are currently developing, innovative immersion schools that are not listed here. These efforts are bringing indigenous languages back to life and restoring cultural solidarity and kinship.

Development of an Ethnobotany Curriculum

My pursuit of an ethnobotany curriculum originated from my personal desire to discover my own heritage and identity as an Anishinaabe person. The passion that fueled my work stemmed from the life of my mother, Rita Theresa Wassegijig, who had spent nine years of her youth, from age 8 to 17, in a Catholic residential school in Spanish, Ontario. It was there that she was severed from her language and cultural identity because of the assimilation policies of both the church and government of Canada. Punishment was rendered daily to those children who spoke their native tongues within the institution. These policies were regarded to be in the best interest of native children as they evolved into civilized society. They were stripped of their ancestral languages and cultural identity, which were replaced with English, Christianity and a trade skill. Eventually, my mother, like many other native children in her generation, ceased speaking the language in her youth, adopted the Catholic faith and became a seamstress. I felt that my work in developing an ethnobotany curriculum in the Anishinaabe language contributed to the reversal of the cultural damage that was inflicted upon those

Native American children, and their children's children, during that dark period in American history.

In my first semester as a biology faculty member at Leech Lake Tribal College, I enrolled in an Ojibwe language course taught by one of my colleagues. The language course gave me a working knowledge of the mechanics of the language, which has a very different linguistic structure than the English language. I also earned the respect of my students because I was sitting in class along with them, making as many mistakes as they were. Equality, as opposed to hierarchy, is highly respected in the Native communities. The course also helped me in the process of translating some of the more complex names and phrases pertaining to plants and ecology.

I acquired a dictionary in the Ojibwe language and began the tedious work of gleaning the words and phrases from each page that would make up the foundation of the ethnobotany curriculum. One of the first dictionaries published on the Ojibwe language was written in 1835 by Frederic Baraga, a Jesuit missionary. The early missionaries in that time period worked hard to learn and phonetically record the indigenous languages in written form. It wasn't until the late 1800s that a new school of thought evolved among the European missionaries who believed indigenous languages and lifeways must be terminated and replaced with Christianity and English. Luckily, the works of Frederic Baraga were preserved and still exist today as a resource for students of the Ojibwe language. Other more contemporary dictionaries in the Ojibwe language are the *Eastern Ojibwa-Chippewa-Ottawa Dictionary* by Richard A. Rhodes (1985) and *A Concise Dictionary of Minnesota Ojibwe* by John Nichols and Earl Nyholm (1995). Other tribal languages were preserved in written form by early missionaries in the 1800s. The work of creating new dictionaries and language curricula is being undertaken today by indigenous peoples themselves, and not members of the clergy.

Luckily, there are scholarly works on the ethnobotanical knowledge of the Anishinaabe. One of the books that has become a bible for Ojibwe ethnobotanists is *How Indians Use Wild Plants for Food, Medicine and Crafts* by Frances Densmore, which was first published in 1928 and reprinted in book format in 1974; it continues to be a cornerstone book for ethnobotany studies in Ojibwe language. Another great reference book is *Plants Used by the Great Lakes Ojibwa* by James Meeker, Joan Elias and John Heim from the Great Lakes Indian Fish and Wildlife Commission (GLIFWC) in Odanah, Wisconsin. This reference is a compilation of the earlier ethnographic studies of Frances Densmore, Huron Smith and other ethnographers who lived among the early Anishinaabe communities in the late 1800s and recorded as much knowledge and language as possible. Many of these historical works must be carefully read keeping in mind that these ethnographers may or may not have had a complete understanding of the language or the cultural nuances that they were recording at the time. For example, Frances Densmore recorded the names of plants used as dyes which, unfortunately, do not work. But, overall, the historical references are vital to building an ethno-botany curriculum.

Other ethnobotanical works from different tribal perspectives are: *Uses of Plants by the Indians of the Missouri River Region* by Melvin R. Gilmore, *Montana Native Plants and Early Peoples* by Jeff Hart, and *Medicinal Wild Plants of the Prairie* by Kelly Kindscher. Nancy J. Turner has several books on the ethnobotany of aboriginal peoples of British Columbia. Daniel Moerman of the University of Michigan at Dearborn created *Native American Ethnobotany*, which is an excellent comprehensive reference resource for Native North American ethnobotany.

The core of the ethnobotany curriculum consists of:

1. identifying the plant names in Ojibwe, Latin and common names, both in the classroom and in the field;
2. learning the traditional uses of plants, including traditional harvesting methods;
3. learning the cultural protocols regarding medicinal and ceremonial plants.

I found that tribal college students are very enthusiastic about learning the plants from their own cultural perspectives. From my observations, most Native students want to learn their ancestral languages for their own spiritual growth and identity, although psychological roadblocks do exist that originate from family attitudes and cultural oppression, a reality that stems from federal boarding school experience. I have seen that academic confidence and self-assurance can grow from their success in learning the complexities of their ancestral language.

One important point that I make in the ethnobotany course is that tribal medicinal knowledge is not taught in an academic setting. In the Anishinaabe culture, the Midewewin Society is a gathering of spiritual healers, shamans, and elders, people versed in the art of healing and ceremony, who pass on this knowledge within the tribe. The knowledge of the plants is powerful and must be conveyed to students through ceremonial protocol and integrity. People who do not attain the ethical and spiritual teachings incorporated into this knowledge can do harm to other people or to the medicines themselves, as seen with the over-exploitation of Echinacea in the northern plains. In many indigenous societies, the plant world is the interface between humans and the spirit world. Medicinal plants, hallucinogenic plants, and spiritual plants such as love charms and smudges, are bridges between the physical and spiritual realities. Therefore, in the classroom, we only talk about the identification of medicinal plants and how they are or were used, but we restrict the knowledge of remedies and dosages of particular medicinal plants. Obtaining the knowledge of healing is regarded as a spiritual path and must be sought by the individual.

Students are also fascinated by the parallels between indigenous knowledge and Western science and technology, thus creating an interest in the STEM disciplines. In the spring of 2000, Leech Lake Tribal College, University of Cincinnati, and NASA Glenn Research Center developed the Native American Remote Sensing Distance Education Prototype (NARSDEP) where tribal college students were able to analyze natural stands of wild rice using Landsat-7 satellite multispectral imagery. Using these satellite images of the reservation, students were able to identify and quantify wild rice beds from year to year, a direct connection between technology and their knowledge of wild rice. Students were also able to see space-oriented images of their homelands, which gave them new perspectives on how technology could be used within their communities. One proposed project was to identify and label place names in the Ojibwe language using GIS programming.

SACRED PLACE NAMES

Sacred place names mark the history of a people with the landscape. Two well-known sacred islands of the Anishinaabe are Manitoulin Island in Ontario which is pronounced as "Manido minising—Island of the Spirits" and Madeline Island in Wisconsin which is named "Mooningwanekaaning—Island of the Northern Flicker". Sacred place names are usually held in secret within tribal communities and the locations of sacred sites are unmarked. There have been cases in the past where sacred sites have been exploited and desecrated; therefore, Native peoples honor these sites in silence in an effort to preserve the sacredness for their community. This knowledge of sacred sites is also vital for the upcoming generations of young people which will promote their spiritual connections with their ancestral homelands.

ETHNOBOTANY FOR THE 21ST CENTURY

So why study ethnobotany? Why have sacred names? The study of ethnobotany can contribute to the restoration of the ecological wisdom of an indigenous culture. People that have a long tenure within a particular region have gained much knowledge about the ecology of place. That knowledge is preserved in the names characterizing the plants, animals, landscapes and climate. The botanical knowledge of indigenous peoples contains cultural values, ethics, sacredness and legends, aspects that are not found in objectified Western science. These aspects of indigenous knowledge allow people to identify with their surroundings and thus create a better stewardship with the earth. The ecological knowledge that was lost because of federal boarding school era may be recovered once again through diligent pursuit of the indigenous languages.

Combining indigenous plant knowledge with science and technology expands the breadth of understanding of plants and ecology, an understanding unlike that of our indigenous ancestors. I do not believe that Western science conflicts with indigenous knowledge, although historically the expansion of Western civilization has adversely impacted indigenous societies globally. Instead, I see the possibility of new technologies and paradigms that can evolve as a result of this integration of science and indigenous knowledge. The combination of these two bodies of knowledge will be valuable in addressing the future problems facing tribal communities, especially the challenge of global climate change.

The children of indigenous communities will soon be faced with the challenges of climate change. According to the Intergovernmental Panel on Climate Change (IPCC), low income and indigenous communities will be more adversely impacted than any other group. I am not so pessimistic about indigenous communities because of their culture of adaptability and sustainability. Indigenous cultures are not as technologically advanced as metropolitan societies, but are far more resilient and adaptable, and they understand the dynamics of their homelands much more intimately.

Shifts in water resources and vegetation will be the bio-indicators of an altered climate. Some regions of the country will experience greening, while others will experience drought. All organic life that depends on the plants (animals, birds, insects and human beings) will shift according to shifting patterns in vegetation, as told in the Creation Story by Anishinaabe elder Basil Johnston in the book, *Ojibway Heritage*. In the Ojibwe language, we know that arrowhead is an aquatic food plant named "Waabiziipin—White Swan potato". From an Ojibwe cultural context, the relationship between the migrating white swans and this aquatic plant is recorded in the name. If shifts in climate alter the migratory patterns of white swans and they are no longer seen in Minnesota, that ecological relationship will still be preserved in the language.

Wild rice, a northern aquatic grass which yields a grain high in carbohydrates, may be adversely impacted by a changing climate because of its sensitivity to water fluctuations. Wild rice is known as "Minoomin—the good seed" and is a sacred plant of the Anishinaabe people. Diminishing stands of wild rice will have detrimental effects on the culture and economy of the Anishinaabe people who depend on the wild rice harvest in the autumn. Therefore, it is imperative that Anishinaabe people understand their relationship to wild rice and reacquaint themselves with its ecology in order to better cope with a changing ecosystem. Many other tribal nations will be faced with the problems of climate change, especially those communities that still live off of the land. Their knowledge of the plants and climate is imperative to their physical survival. Indigenous peoples of the Arctic as well as the Pacific islands are already experiencing the effects of climate change, while indigenous peoples of the temperate and tropical latitudes are just beginning to witness changes to their homelands.

Language is the spiritual glue that can build community cohesion and connect people to the land. The names of plants and places define the relationship between land and people. The cultural values, woven into the language, determine if our relationship to the earth is respectful and sustainable. Many indigenous languages survived assimilative annihilation, many did not. Those that did survive may become stronger and more vibrant than before. Ecological wisdom and knowledge will spring forth from those young minds that embrace their indigenous languages and share them with the world.

From 1995 to 2008, Michael Price served as chair of the math and science department at Leech Lake Tribal College in Cass Lake, Minnesota.

It Is Not Necessary For Eagles To Be Crows

Integrating Culture In Stem Programs At Sitting Bull College

Jeremy Guinn

The question for many tribal college STEM instructors is this: Are we training scientists who just happen to be Native American, or are we producing Native American scientists who use modern scientific concepts and their unique cultural perspectives to enhance the scientific community and benefit all people? *Tatanka Iyotanke's* (Sitting Bull) words serve as a guide to incorporating the Lakota/Dakota culture into STEM programs at Sitting Bull College. Our goal is not to change our Native American students into standard scientists; instead, we are enhancing the scientific community and the educational capital of the Standing Rock Reservation by educating students who understand the place of science within their cultural worldview. This chapter describes the ongoing and evolving process of integrating traditional knowledge into STEM courses and the environmental science program at Sitting Bull College.

Opportunities

When attempting to develop innovative STEM programs and courses that are enhanced with cultural content, we are faced with many challenges. One of the most relevant challenges is accreditation and transferability of cultural-based courses. Although the tribal college community may see the importance of cultural integration in certain courses, the transfer university may not. While it is intellectually appealing to develop a pure Native science curriculum, the applicability for our students—whether they are transferring or entering the job market—is often not present. For these reasons, we have not developed a full Native science degree program; instead, we have incorporated Lakota/Dakota culture into each of our courses and fully integrated culture in several *ethno-courses*. The result is a program that is attractive to tribal members, is scientifically rigorous, and enhances the traditional knowledge of our students and faculty.

For non-Native faculty members, it is often intimidating to incorporate even a single cultural example, not to mention developing a full culturally-based course. STEM faculty at a tribal college should be open to new ideas and interested in continuing their own education in their chosen profession. They should also show an interest in the culture of the people they serve. A lack of cultural knowledge is often a key to their initial trepidation. To address these issues, we took several steps toward making it easier for faculty to learn more about the tribe's culture by taking courses and pursuing a degree in Native American Studies. Both of the faculty members in the environmental science program have taken advantage of these opportunities and obtained their A.S. degrees in 2008. The information that they obtained during this course of study facilitates the integration of cultural content into their courses in a number of ways. Learning the proper pronunciation and usage of just a few animal names provides an initial means of connecting a course to the culture. More advanced courses increase the cultural content dramatically through language use and also through concepts related to tribal history, law, and literature.

Students enter our programs with a wide range of backgrounds in academics and in traditional culture. There is an obvious bell-shaped curve of traditional experience with some students being very active in traditional culture, others having relatively no experience, and most students falling somewhere between. Introducing these students to traditional concepts that are new to them and having them share whatever stories they know is very important in their development as community and classroom leaders.

How to Identify Potential Content

The cultural content of your courses is of prime importance and should be reviewed for accuracy and appropriateness before incorporation into your curricula. Publications are a good place to start when you first begin to bring culture into courses; however, they should be reviewed by someone who is knowledgeable about the culture. The quality and amount of published information varies dramatically according to the tribe(s) of concern. The published accounts offer written, documented information that is in an easily incorporated format. However, many books about Native American communities and traditions were written from external perspectives and some of the interpretations of events or ceremonies are either incorrect or are not appropriate for open discussion. It is always preferable to check with someone who knows before using it in class—it will save a lot of stress and embarrassment.

The best source of cultural information, and the best source of new and interesting information, comes from the elders in your community. This is sometimes the most difficult and time-consuming kind of information to obtain, however. It is important that you approach elders with respect and remember that you may not be ready to learn everything they know. Ask your questions and use what they give you with permission, but understand that you may not have all the pieces of the puzzle the first time that you talk with them. Always keep in mind that you are doing this for your students and never publish anything without the elder's (and sometimes the elder's family's) full support and consent.

In some cultures, there are specific protocols for knowing and telling certain stories. If you are not the proper person to tell a specific story, then maybe it's better to have the elder come to the class to tell the story, or perhaps, it is not appropriate for the story to be told to a general audience at all. There are times when, although it would make a great class discussion, you will have to just let a topic go in order to be respectful of the culture. In the end, maintaining a respect for the protocols will benefit your program and your students through strengthening your community relationships.

STRATIFICATION OF CULTURAL INTEGRATION

Our success has been in an ability to be patient in integrating culture into our programs and in identifying courses that are more adaptable to a full cultural integration. A stratified hierarchy of cultural integration allows us to develop courses, research projects, outreach programs, and community service projects that are feasible financially, attractive to a range of potential students, and culturally appropriate. Cultural integration has been addressed in four main areas of our college experience and includes both curricular and extracurricular activities. We have made commitments to the culture in (1) courses, (2) research projects, (3) outreach programs, and (4) community service activities. Within each of these areas, there are different levels of cultural integration. The goal is to continually increase the relevant cultural content in each area by adding new modules, developing new cultural resources, and producing higher quality cultural and scientific programs. The key is always to find the link between the cultural content and the most appropriate course content.

Courses and Programs

Each course offered at Sitting Bull College is required to have at least one "culturally-relevant activity." This is often a simple basic assignment or presentation, but may be more involved for other courses. It is easier for some faculty to develop these activities because of their experience and because of their individual courses; however, a cultural connection can be found in each course if the instructor does some background research. Within STEM courses, it is typically easier to develop specific modules for a particular course. In earth science courses, we discuss multiple earth-creation stories from many different cultures and examine how those stories reflect the modern scientific view of creation. We often find that many traditional stories have concepts similar to those developed by Western science. This type of course, with only a few isolated cultural activities, represents the beginning level of cultural integration.

Within STEM courses, the next step is to develop hybrid courses, which are approximately 50 percent pure science content and 50 percent culturally-based content relating directly to course materials. Many wildlife related courses provide prime opportunities to address cultural issues throughout the course. Using traditional names for wild animals is a good place to start. We build on this by defining the traditional words within the Lakota name of the animal to get more information about species' morphology, behavior, or relationships. We can do the same thing with the scientific name. Just utilizing the names for the species often brings new enlightenment about the animal we are describing and provides the spark for doing more interesting investigations. Many traditional stories utilize key characteristics of a species' behavior. We often read the stories first, and then move into how that behavioral trait affects the survival or reproductive success of a particular population. In other geoscience courses, we have utilized stories comparing the fossil legends of Native Americans to introduce and investigate the evolution of our understanding of fossilized dinosaur bones and stratigraphy. In this case, traditional stories were much closer to what we consider the truth about these bones today than the initial European ideas. The understanding of the environment and ecological processes expressed in these stories is fundamentally more advanced than traditional Western science.

The final level is represented by full culture-based courses, such as Ethnobotany. Ethnobotany was originally offered solely as a Native American Studies course. However, the course was adapted by the addition of a full laboratory section that focuses on morphology and chemistry so that it is now also offered for credit as a botany or plant sciences lab credit. Ethnobotany served as a model for developing other culturally-based science courses. These courses are typically offered as a laboratory science course so that students outside of STEM majors can take them to fulfill general education requirements. Ethno-courses fill a distinct niche within our campus by providing solid science foundations and an exciting and interesting culture-based course for majors and non-majors. Another culture-based science course is Birds and Culture, a combination of a traditional ornithology course and a bird symbology course. The course utilizes traditional images, stories, and usages of birds to develop the concepts of ornithology. Offered at the 200-level, Birds and Culture focuses on bird identification (including classification and morphology) and the structure, function, and coloration of feathers while examining traditional stories which provide the basis for discussions about migration, nesting behavior, and other characteristics.

Research Projects

Similarly, we have developed a stratification of cultural integration within research programs. Our student research opportunities have ranged from pure culturally-driven research, to hybrid projects, to appropriate research with culturally important species. The variety of cultural integration in research programs has been based on scientific opportunity, student questions about cultural use of plants and animal stories, and respect for specific cultural protocols. Of prime importance is the protection of natural resources on tribal lands. Studies on air, water, and soil contamination have been particularly attractive to our students.

With proper review and approval, we have developed several research programs that involve culturally important species. The programs within this level of cultural integration are primarily concerned with surveying and monitoring the populations of these species for basic information, but not investigating a particular cultural aspect. These projects include a winter roadside survey for raptors. Many species of hawk and eagle feathers are utilized by the Lakota/Dakota for a variety of purposes. Our survey work has identified a trend in migration that could be related to climate change. Another project involved surveying for turtles on Standing Rock to identify their occurrence and distribution. Turtles were utilized in many ways by the Lakota/Dakota. We identified a turtle species that had never been reported in North Dakota.

Most of our research programs have a cultural foundation. In addition to initial turtle surveys, we are now investigating other questions that have been brought to us through traditional stories or by community members. This includes study of the turtle's winter behavior and movements and particular aspects of the shell morphology. These questions are exciting for our students and could lead to advances in currently accepted ideas about turtles in our region. It is an evolution of our research program and also our cultural integration program. Other studies concentrate on pollution in traditional waterways. We have investigated water quality and mercury levels in fish taken from popular fishing areas. Our students feel a strong pull to protect their natural resources and these projects are viewed as cultural because they protect the quality of their traditional lands.

The classification, *full culture-driven research program*, is defined as a project based on a cultural question from a student or community member that is significant to the Lakota/Dakota culture. For example, one research project investigated the uptake of heavy metals by traditional plants, such as wild turnip (*tinpsila*). *Tinpsila* were traditionally utilized in soups and other meals and *tinpsila*-hunting continues to be a major activity for a portion of the population on the Standing Rock Reservation. *Tinpsila* is also eaten in large quantities during the prime season, which means that people may be exposed to high doses of contaminants if the plant actively stores heavy metals in the roots.

Outreach Programs

The college is active in engaging local elementary and secondary schools in specific programs. Occasionally, we are invited to speak on a particular topic, but more often we are invited to come and speak about any topic. Our outreach programs also reflect a stratified design and run from full cultural presentations to simply speaking about species that are culturally significant. We have been improving our presentations so that we do not miss opportunities to present cultural connections.

When asked to present about a specific topic, such as bird identification for special high school science competitions, it is often necessary to stay very close to the topic that the teacher requests. In these cases, our outreach programs have limited cultural content. However, it is possible to tie in a few examples if we know the material and the traditional stories relating to the content without wasting the teacher's class time. More often, we are able to offer presentations about our research programs in which we provide activities related to the methods and results of our research that also make connections to the culture. For example, when discussing water quality research, it is easy to transition into discussions about the food web and the culturally important animals that will be affected by degraded water and destroyed habitat.

We have had the opportunity to offer several full traditional presentations based on our animal research. Primarily, we have concentrated on traditional stories and use of turtles and plants. These programs are particularly effective for younger audiences. They are also very effective if the undergraduate students that participated in the research are also involved in the outreach program. One particularly popular presentation was presented by two students. One student described all the turtle species on Standing Rock Reservation using mounted photographs of each species and their habitats and the other student read traditional stories about turtles and described connections between the stories and what she learned from our research.

Community Service Projects

As active members of our program, we insist that our students participate in our community service projects. Stratification can also be observed in these projects, which range from participating in ceremonies to picking up trash from specific culturally-important sites.

Some activities are very basic, including participating in clean-up days in the community and around campus. These activities are also about taking care of Mother Earth and protecting the natural resources of traditional lands. One particular event included unloading a semi-truck delivery and packaging Thanksgiving and Christmas meals for the elderly. This reflects the traditional esteem for elders and the position they hold in traditional Lakota/Dakota society.

We are also active in "sponsoring" opportunities for students to participate in traditional activities. A sponsorship may be as simple as asking permission to invite our students to participate and making sure that everyone in the program knows about the event. In other cases, it may be that the students/faculty actually do some of the groundwork (cutting wood, hauling rocks, etc.) that will make it easier on the person conducting the ceremony. Although they may be interested, many students do not have the opportunity to participate in certain activities simply because their family or immediate relatives were not raised in a traditional manner. By offering these opportunities, we have made available some essential cultural experiences to a much wider audience of Lakota/Dakota students. By participating in these ceremonies, the students will have a better connection to the cultural concepts that we are attempting to integrate into our courses and a wider foundation of experiences from which to draw later in life. Some of these events include buffalo ceremonies, sweat lodge ceremonies, and discussions with elders on a variety of traditional topics. Students also help prepare and butcher a buffalo for the annual Sitting Bull College pow-wow.

PERSONAL EXPERIENCE

Soon after I was hired at Sitting Bull College, I was asked to develop a full culturally-based course as part of a grant to enhance STEM programs at the college. This was an interesting and imposing challenge for me, as I was relatively new to this region of the country and completely unfamiliar with Lakota culture and life on the reservation. I found this to be a particularly daunting task, but also very intellectually intriguing. On one hand, I was excited about the amazing opportunity to learn more about the culture. On the other hand, how was I going to develop and teach a culturally-based program when I did not have any experience or prior knowledge about the culture? Below are some comments and suggestions that helped me along the way.

I quickly found that a sincere interest in another person's culture is usually well-received. I would, however, suggest that course development only be attempted by instructors who have an honest interest in the people and culture of the community. If they don't, the process of trying to develop a course will be a long, arduous journey. It does no good to force your faculty members into developing a culturally-based course. In fact, forcing an unmotivated faculty member into offering this type of course will likely damage the college's relationship with *its* students and community.

Respect and humility are two huge character traits that should dictate your relationships throughout the process of developing and teaching a culturally-based course. One of the most important ideas to remember is that it is not your privilege to know everything about the culture. You will need to rely on many people to help you along the way, but do not be too aggressive with your questioning. No one likes their intimate, personal beliefs to be pried into by someone digging for information. There is a fine line between being persistent to get the information you need for the course and knowing when to withdraw from a line of questioning. Build a few trusting personal relationships first so that people understand that your questions reflect a respectful curiosity about them and their heritage.

Be patient. If you are completely new to the area and culture, developing a culturally-based course might take you three or more years, depending on a variety of factors. I suggest starting with foundation reading, if available. Other educators and co-workers are valuable resources. Many of your co-workers are members of the culture and will be able to answer most of your questions or at least point you in the right direction to find the answer. It is also likely that there are many people around you that were not raised in the culture. At some point, these people had to learn some things about the culture or they probably would not still be employed at your institution. Give special attention to those who seem to have good relationships with people in the community. These are the people who will likely be the most sympathetic and helpful in your quest for knowledge about the culture.

Next, begin to delve a little deeper into the culture. Again, take things slowly, but at some point you need to get vital information about your course material or move on to the next subject. Be conscious of your questions when you do not understand what people are talking about. Inquire about the language, take a course or several courses on the culture if offered, and read more about the history of the people. Soon you will find that you know more of the facts about the history of the reservation than the average person in the community. One of the most important steps in developing the course is asking for stories—oral traditions—from the people. I began collecting stories about two years prior to first offering the course and still make a concerted effort to bring in more stories.

Finally, talk to the elders of the community and invite the elders to tell their stories directly to the class. Contact with the elders is not always easy to accomplish, and it can be stressful the first few times, but I think it is a vital step in the process that should not be ignored. For many peoples, the elders are the holders of the culture. It is only right that they should have a part in developing the curricula of a culturally-based course. I have found many of the local elders to be very willing to speak to my classes and help in any way. Student response to elders in the classroom is remarkable. Elder presentations are usually highlights of the semester.

Do not attempt to teach outside of your specialty. Many of us teaching at institutions where culturally-based courses are attractive teach a high load of contact hours and often teach courses slightly outside of our natural area of expertise. I strongly discourage trying to develop a culturally-based course outside of your personal specialty, especially if you are developing your first cultural course.

Many issues became apparent when speaking to locals and trying to decipher some of the oral traditions. In many instances, I would have been completely lost if I did not have a very strong background in ornithology. For instance, many of the common names for birds have changed over the last century and there are many local names for the same species. Many of the oral traditions use older names and references. These stories would have been useless to me if I did not know a little about the history of bird names in this part of the country.

For instance, in my particular field, many of the oral traditions focus on the Spotted Eagle. This was a problem for me because we have only two eagle species in the Northern Plains: Bald Eagles and Golden Eagles. These birds have completely different behaviors and usually live in different habitats. So, what is the Spotted Eagle? The stories actually refer to the immature birds of either species, which have mottled white and brown/black plumage and look very similar to each other. Usually there is a habitat reference or behavioral trait described in the story that allows species identification to be made. So in discussing the Spotted Eagle stories, students also learn how to identify adult and immature eagles and learn their habitat and behaviors. They also have a better idea of where their own ceremonial feathers originate.

If you insist on trying to develop a culturally-based course outside of your specialty, be sure to enlist at least one expert in the field to review you scientific content. Of course, I did not heed this good advice and attempted to develop a culturally-based earth science/geology course. After spinning my wheels for several semesters, I had to go back and teach myself more geology, talk to a local geologist and a paleontologist, develop a working relationship with the tribe's archaeologist, and redo much of the cultural research I had already done, but did not fully understand.

Students are a great source of information. They can reach a much more diverse group of people than a single instructor. Their help in gathering stories has been invaluable to my process. Not only do they bring in stories about their culture, they also bring in varying viewpoints within the tribe, and have introduced me to some of my best teaching resources. Prior to teaching the culturally-based course, I enlisted students in other courses to develop a report on at least one story from their family that was relevant to birds. Students turned in audiotaped interviews, videos of their families and friends, and transcriptions of stories. I utilized these materials (with permission) as a foundation for developing the course.

This foundation was also an important reference when obtaining approval from my curriculum committee. One of the obvious and valid questions that you are likely to receive—whether you are Native or non-Native is, "Why do you think you are qualified to teach this course?" It was a difficult question, but one that needs to be addressed by anyone attempting to teach a culturally-based course. Without the log of stories, traditional names, and uses of birds, I really would have had nothing to stand on when attempting to prove my ability to teach a culturally-based course.

One mistake that I made early in developing the course was to concentrate solely on the culture of the majority of my students. While this is the overall objective, I soon learned that many of my students were fascinated by discussions of other cultures, as well. They like hearing oral traditions from other tribes around the world and comparing them to their own stories. In addition, many of the students that I assumed were from the culture of the community were actually Native students from tribes across the country. Their stories add a great deal to the discussions in these courses. Remember to always acknowledge the culture that you are discussing, so that it is clear which people you are speaking about.

It is especially gratifying for me as a non-Native person to feel comfortable and accepted within the community to the point that they trust me teaching certain aspects of their culture to their children. Learning more about the culture has been one of the most rewarding parts of my life. It has improved my life mentally, spiritually, and emotionally. I have learned a great deal about the behavior and characteristics of living animals and fossils from listening to the elders speak in my classes. These ideas produce many new research questions that I would have never considered without their stories. Additionally, these courses serve as a storehouse for these traditional stories from around the reservation.

CONCLUSIONS

The benefits of integrating culture into the curricula are enormous. Students receive an education that is far beyond what they would receive at a typical university. They graduate with positive feelings about who they are and a confidence in their scientific knowledge. Incorporating elders into classroom lectures enhances the bond between the college and the community and between the younger and older generations.

Cultural integration is about infusing the curricula with culture. It is difficult to assess cultural integration in terms of the number of graduates because cultural integration has occurred alongside other projects that all share the larger goal of increasing the number of Native American STEM students and graduates. We know that cultural content is important and interesting to our students, but it is difficult to quantify the initial impact of these efforts. The primary challenge is lack of time and cultural knowledge of those developing or teaching the courses. It takes a great deal of personal time and personal effort to develop an effective culturally-based course.

Our STEM programs are growing and the quality of student preparation, as measured in their products, is outstanding. Several students are presenting their research at regional and national scientific meetings on a routine basis, and we recently submitted three manuscripts for publication in peer-reviewed scientific journals. Many of our graduates are now working in science-related positions with local and regional environmental agencies and/or beginning their graduate degree programs. Their contributions to the scientific community are already happening and we expect to see more out of each of them. This is the primary way that we measure the initial success of our efforts to make our programs more culturally relevant and empowering for our students.

Dr. Jeremy Guinn is an Environmental Science instructor at Sitting Bull College, which is located on the Standing Rock Reservation in Fort Yates, North Dakota. He specializes in raptor research, wildlife management, telemetry, and GIS.

Cultural Integration at
Northwest Indian College

An Experience of Cultural
Restoration

Cheryl Crazy Bull

Northwest Indian College (NWIC), chartered by the Lummi Nation, has its main campus on the Lummi homelands in the northwest corner of Washington with extended campus sites at other locations in Washington and Idaho. After serving as a two year degree granting institution for nearly 25 years, NWIC recently became a candidate for accreditation at the baccalaureate degree granting level. The first degree program chosen for implementation is the Native Environmental Science (NES) bachelor of science. This new degree has two tracks—one in environmental science with an emphasis on basic environmental science proficiency and the other as an interdisciplinary concentration program. The concentration is a more flexible but equally rigorous track that requires students to select a specific topic for study. The concentration allows students to design an individualized program of study mentored by a committee.

In the context of developing and delivering the curriculum associated with this degree, Northwest Indian College faculty and administrators expanded allocation of resources toward cultural integration within the context of our mission to promote indigenous self-determination and knowledge. The college's institutional cultural outcomes, designed by faculty and academic administrators with input from students and the tribal community, are designed to provide students with a sense of place and an understanding of what it is to be a people.

Sharon Kinley, director of the Coast Salish Institute and a Native Studies faculty member at Northwest Indian College, shares the vision of cultural integration at NWIC and in particular for the Native Environmental Science program:

> I believe that we are performing acts of decolonization by giving our students access to their tribal knowledge. We are adding experiences

and knowledge back rather then taking something away from our students or leaving a vacant space. We are helping students relearn their personal and community history. We are helping them regain their connections to the land.

Historical Experience

Northwest Indian College has a long history of examination, practice, and use of cultural integration strategies. Noteworthy to this discussion is the programming associated with the National Science Foundation-funded Tribal Environmental Natural Resource Management Program (TENRM) and the Tribal Colleges and Universities Program (TCUP). These programs developed a strong foundation of cultural learning, faculty development and instructional resources that lend themselves to our current academic programs and instructional strategies.

The Tribal Environmental Natural Resource Management Program provided a unique cohort-based learning community educational model integrating values and perspectives of tribal people with an environmental studies program. Interdisciplinary thematic courses, team-teaching, a non-abandonment policy in support of student success, and research were all part of the program. The Tribal Colleges and Universities Program expanded the fundamental principles of the TENRM program of integrating Native perspectives and Western knowledge to include basic skills development. An emphasis on core first year experience activities occurred with TCUP. Both programs provide a solid foundation of environmental education, inclusion of Native knowledge, and collaborative teaching and learning practices that inform the college's Native Environmental Science program.

Context for Discussion

Our approach for this discussion is to examine the expectations, experiences, and responsibilities of the major participants in cultural integration, including Native faculty, cultural resource people, non-Native faculty, and students. We also share the experiences of the academic leadership of the college as they promote and evaluate cultural integration strategies. Following this discussion, we provide recommendations and advice for administrators and faculty of other tribal colleges as well as other higher education institutions involved in cultural integration.

Research associated with the development of this chapter also aided Northwest Indian College in developing its next steps as we continue our path of full cultural integration.

Cultural integration can be an elusive descriptor of the teaching and learning experience both from the faculty and student perspectives at a tribal college. There are constraints on cultural education. These constraints are primarily the result of the natural limitations of time and opportunity as well as the philosophical intentions of tribal people in their willingness to share indigenous knowledge in formal educational settings. Identification of what is cultural integration is a developing understanding gained over time by both students and staff. Surface cultural integration, for example, might be a class in the techniques of basketry or song and dance whereas deep cultural integration would be the study of the teachings associated with all aspects of weaving or of the songs and dances that are being taught. Symbolism and meaning are the source of learning in the deep culture experience.

The leadership of NWIC, including the president, is influenced in their beliefs about cultural integration by the writings of Vine Deloria, Jr., Elizabeth Cook-Lynn and Linda Tuwahi Smith in their many discussions of the role of Native studies. This in turn influences the institutional climate and practices pertaining to cultural integration. Faculty members are especially influenced by contemporary Native scholars such as Daniel Wildcat, Gregory Cajete and Billy Frank, Jr.

In *New Indian Old Wars* (University of Illinois, 2007) Elizabeth Cook-Lynn discusses the vital necessity of empowerment as the basis of Indian studies research, curriculum development, and instruction. The experience of empowerment for NWIC students will arise out of the focus on indigenousness and sovereignty—concepts that Cook-Lynn says inform the experiences of tribal societies, influence the interpretation of those experiences and our evaluation of those experiences. Our oral traditions and our sense of place are not mythology—they are the knowledge that describes our origins and our specific human experiences as tribal people.

Like all tribal colleges, NWIC's purposes include providing students with a solid "Western" education, exposing them to relevant information that ensures their capability to perform in jobs in their chosen professions. For our purposes, we define "Western" education as that which is derived from the knowledge and experiences of mainstream society and which is intended to help us navigate that society, particularly in the job market. Jobs in the tribal environmental stewardship fields, such as fisheries, natural resources, environmental protection and forestry, require a well balanced education with effective Native-based and technical skills. Our graduates must be able to protect our resources in the context of tribal sovereignty and cultural knowledge while managing resources in the context of contemporary systems.

CULTURAL LEARNING

The intention of cultural integration is, of course, to promote cultural learning so the student gains Western knowledge and, more importantly, becomes more grounded in and knowledgeable of tribal teachings. To this end, faculty and administrators at NWIC have identified ways in which cultural learning can occur in our academic programs and courses:

- Through the opportunity to practice cultural experiences, such as going fishing or clamming, speaking before elders, or walking in the forests.
- Through studying a topic of tribal interest, such as lab experiences that focus on the student's place—land, water, and climate. Instructors identified that the ability to work with students in their contemporary place allows non-Native faculty to participate with cultural integration without having to acquire extensive historical knowledge.
- Through assisting the student in "capturing" and integrating their own experiences such as fishing, tribal rights issues and socio-economic experiences within their educational experience at NWIC. This process validates the student's cultural knowledge and practices, which is an important aspect of the NWIC mission. It also has the additional outcome of helping students understand the different ways that tribal people teach, acquire and maintain tribal knowledge.
- Through the use of written materials published as the result of research in and about tribes and tribal communities. Faculty feel that it is important and necessary to recognize that there are many Native and non-Native writers who have produced materials of value to student learning.

Cultural integration at NWIC is part of our understanding that culture is a multi-layered experience and that exploration of culture in a structured educational environment is an imperfect and incomplete experience. We also recognize that what is taught matters particularly in aspects of deep culture, such as relationships with creation, family relationships, and traditional spiritual knowledge. In Coast Salish and other Pacific Northwest tribal communities, spiritual, private and family knowledge are not taught in institutional settings without explicit permission. Non-Native faculty (or even Native people not from Coast Salish cultures) with no or limited understanding of how sharing occurs in a tribal community are often unsure of how to navigate through or respond to this situation.

From the student perspective issues of diversity of tribal affiliation could be a consideration when instructors strive for cultural integration in their courses. Sometimes, students are unsure of how a particular learning experience informs their education as a citizen of a particular tribal nation. Both faculty and students benefit from the ability to make connections across tribal place-based knowledge.

NWIC faculty and academic leaders consider it an important student outcome to develop the ability to interpret local place-based learning to their own tribal and personal experience.

Spontaneous Cultural Integration

Faculty identified that the most successful cultural integration occurred spontaneously in the classroom and in the field from the students through the students' prior knowledge and through the connections that students make in their learning. Students generate connections between their life knowledge and the course content. The same experience can occur when a cultural resource person or Native faculty member makes a connection in conversation or an educational setting about a STEM topic.

It appears that the success of spontaneous integration hinges on two factors: (1) student and instructor understanding of course materials and content and (2) the extent to which the instructor can facilitate a discussion that is redirected due to the spontaneous integration experience. Students must be open to the connections between the subject and their own lives and faculty members must help the students identify the relevance of the knowledge to their own lives.

Students will vary as to the extent to which they can individually focus their cultural knowledge on either surface or deep culture integration. A deep understanding of course content is important to the experience of spontaneous integration because the instructor must then be able to draw out the connections that students are making and then must be able to use the integration activity as a means of teaching the materials. Faculty at NWIC identified that knowing when to let students teach is an important skill for a teacher in the classroom where spontaneous integration occurs. An instructor must also develop the ability to recognize when he has reached a point of discomfort with his ability to participate with both planned and spontaneous integration. This ability is deeply rooted in self-reflection and in the willingness of faculty as discussed throughout this chapter.

Planned Cultural Integration

The most commonly identified form of cultural integration is planned integration. This occurs in two primary settings—the classroom and in field-based experiences. Classroom-based experiences are generally pre-identified by the instructor and are described in the course syllabus or outline. Typically they are also included in the instructor's course assessment. Field-based experiences are especially available in science courses. They are also generally pre-identified as part of the course outline. Distinctive place-based experiences reliant upon local cultural resources and materials are often a part of formal cultural integration assignments and projects in courses. Cultural resources could include people, environmental resources and activities, and traditional knowledge.

According to NWIC faculty, access to cultural resource people and availability of related cultural instructional materials are important keys to successful planned integration. Because the majority of STEM faculty at NWIC are not Native, they don't have ready access to cultural knowledge either through experience or education. This cultural knowledge can be either historic or contemporary. In other words, it can be knowledge of how the past informs contemporary education or it can be use of the contemporary environment to connect with traditional knowledge. In any case, non-Native faculty generally must learn their cultural knowledge with Native people using both oral tradition and written materials. Different approaches to this type of learning exist and are often an area of uncertainty for faculty. The dearth of available cultural resource people (with content specific knowledge) as well as written and media resources usually means that the instructor must both research and design cultural integration assignments.

Another factor in successful planned integration is the willingness *and* ability of the faculty member. An instructor at NWIC must be able to identify and integrate materials, often with minimal access to cultural experts in the STEM fields. Most cultural resource experts have expertise in social sciences, such as history and government, and with human services. Instructors working on their own or with the help of others who are knowledgeable about the community must find people with environmental, natural resources, marine science, ecological or other science knowledge or they must find other non-Native faculty with expertise. There is no easy path for the instructor who usually must expend considerable effort to find informants who can assist with curriculum development or can "team-teach" at appropriate times.

Also, because most faculty at NWIC are not trained in the teaching professions (as is true of most faculty who are not teacher educators at other tribal colleges and mainstream institutions), there is no guarantee that a faculty member knows how to design and/or revise curriculum. Often faculty members teach in their content area based on their own prior college experience or with minimal faculty development regarding curriculum strategies. The ability of faculty to write curriculum is enhanced at NWIC through various curriculum writing projects and through faculty development focused on teaching and learning strategies.

Cultural integration in courses is usually generated by faculty desiring an improved and more meaningful educational experience for Native students. Prior to recent developments in assessment and outcome work at NWIC, faculty strived to integrate Native knowledge and experiences through programs such as TENRM and through faculty development opportunities.

Current institutionally supported activities to help instructors with planned integration include:

- Mini-immersions: Three to five faculty members work in teams to participate in immersion activities overseen by the Native faculty in the Coast Salish Institute. This strategy was identified by academic administrators as an approach that both provided access to cultural resources and assisted the "ability" aspect of faculty in the NES program.

- Place-based field trips: These opportunities for students and faculty usually associated with a class are team-taught by Native and non-Native faculty with community members sharing their cultural knowledge, inclusive of elders and with a Native language speaker providing instruction throughout the process.

- Institutional, program and course outcomes: Outcomes ensure an institutional focus on student knowledge, skills and abilities and, in particular, provide a framework for cultural outcomes. Institutional cultural outcomes are focused on both student and faculty competencies. The two college-wide NWIC outcomes are "to be a People" and "a sense of place."

- An emphasis on leadership and effectiveness: Students will be able to articulate the diversity in spirituality, culture and language; articulate their own identity in terms of a sense of place and their people; demonstrate knowledge of Native American and other models of leadership; and demonstrate effective leadership skills. This activity is still being developed.

- Modern and historic Native experiences: NWIC has a teaching and learning initiative funded from multiple sources to support faculty development and continuous improvement. In particular the Woksape Oyate (Intellectual Capacity) Initiative has a Modern and Historic Native Experience component that enhances the foundational knowledge of faculty about Native students and communities. Resources from the programs provided by this activity provide instructors with increased access for integration. For example, a recent workshop on modern issues of Indian identity and population change included a review of available Web based resources from organizations such as the National Museum of American Indians and the National Congress of American Indians.

- Shared strategies among instructors: Faculty also have numerous opportunities to share their integration activities. A few examples of cultural integration in STEM courses are: zoology (study of local fauna in the Lummi Peninsula which is the traditional homelands of the Lummi people); ethno-botany (study of the medicinal properties of traditional plants); and chemistry (study of alcohol properties and their impact on family and individual health in tribal communities; chemical properties of fabric dyes for weaving and sewing projects).

INFLUENCES ON THE CULTURAL INTEGRATION EXPERIENCE

NWIC has a clear mission statement emphasizing tribal self-determination and knowledge. The college's strategic plan, institutional program and course outcomes, program development and assessment processes all intentionally focus on tribal identity and cultural understanding. Considerable institutional resources, including expanded staffing and services in the Coast Salish Institute, are devoted to building our institutional capacity to teach Native Studies and provide cultural integration. The Coast Salish Institute in particular seeks to build instructional resources and programming in support of Lummi and Coast Salish languages and culture.

We also emphasize our place-based mission by providing coursework that is adaptable to the different tribal locations we serve. For example, Ecology of the First People is a core NES course developed to teach students about the origin of their own people from an environmental perspective including where they emerged, their relationships to the natural environment, and their relationships to each other. It includes developing an understanding of the inherent rights and responsibilities that emerge from their place of origin. This course is very adaptable to the location and teachings of our tribal sites in areas such as treaties, acquired rights, political history, and origin stories. It is a very place-based course.

The location of the majority of NWIC's campuses along the coast of the Puget Sound provides a unique opportunity for cultural integration focused on the sea and its river tributaries. While there are many cultural resource people and research projects associated with the marine environment and ecosystems, there are limitations in our capacity to easily translate practical and everyday knowledge into academic courses and assignments. The ability of Native resource people to connect culture across diverse subject matter is a factor in the timely development of culturally integrated materials and assignments. The development of trusting relationships among Native and non-Native faculty and resource people is a foundational experience contributing to successful integration support. Development and maintenance of those relationships takes focus, time and effort.

Because the majority of the STEM faculty at Northwest Indian College are not Native American, issues such as the fear of making a mistake, knowing the appropriateness of materials, or the ability to access a knowledgeable informant influence both the quantity and quality of cultural integration. Instructors identified that their own individual ability to let the student be the teacher, to be adaptable on a daily basis, and to be able to listen and know the issues faced by our students are factors determining the effectiveness of cultural integration. Each instructor is responsible for ensuring the student learns the core Western knowledge expected of someone educated in the subject matter while also responding to the institutional and tribal expectation that the student's cultural knowledge will be enhanced.

FACULTY CHARACTERISTICS

The following characteristics appear necessary for an instructor to successfully participate with integration experiences both in teaching and learning and in materials development:

- Responsiveness to students and the skill to read/know students of different cultures;
- Readiness to integrate cultural information in both attitude and ability to integrate cultural information;
- Deliberate cultivation of the ability to recognize artifacts of assimilation;
- Belief in the value of and willingness to teach from a multi-disciplinary perspective;
- General knowledge base of cultural learning including American Indian history, sociology and political science;
- General knowledge base of Native science knowledge as discussed by such resources as Vine Deloria Jr., Gregory Cajete, Daniel Wildcat, and Winona LaDuke;
- Philosophical belief in the value of both historic and contemporary Native knowledge;
- Prior experience with cultural diversity, tribal communities or with alternative Native curricula (other then only Western science based curricula).

The creation of a safe classroom and institutional climate in support of cross-cultural communication is a work in progress at NWIC. Students need to trust the teacher before they will feel comfortable in sharing their own prior knowledge or exploring how their knowledge informs the course content. Instructors are challenged by the impact of the assimilation process on our understanding of tribal perspectives. Generally, in tribal societies there is specific cultural knowledge possessed by individuals or held in common. Our Native understanding of diversity is that it inherently occurs among tribes and not necessarily within an understanding of cultural practice.

Assimilation and cultural oppression contribute to the promotion of "diverse" views about specific tribal cultural knowledge and practice. We are constantly seeking the right balance between what Native experts might know to be true about our cultural knowledge and how that knowledge has evolved over time. Colonization altered the natural process of knowledge acquisition and sharing in our tribal communities, creating a sense of confusion among tribal people that is a challenge in the instructional process.

Readiness of students to participate in cultural learning and to regain their experience with the land is as important as the willingness and ability of the instructor to teach. Students vary as to their experiences with their culture and in the extent of their tribal identity. STEM faculty and NES students at NWIC are exploring cultural integration together.

Experience of Cultural Integration

Faculty at Northwest Indian College see themselves as consistently improving in their ability to provide culturally integrated materials, experiences and resources. The cultivation of relationships with community and students contribute to the quality of the experience. Many faculty feel that the addition of the concentration option in the NES program enhanced the opportunity for cultural integration because it has broader implications for course choices by students focused on student identification of research and learning interests. Students will need to think deeply about their own goals and work with faculty and community members to focus on those goals.

Faculty who teach the hard sciences such as chemistry, physics and biology have core knowledge that must be transmitted as a foundational experience for students. While faculty are able to integrate the students' experiences into the courses (i.e. alcohol studies in chemistry and fish studies in biology), they still must ensure students meet the science outcomes.

Unique social and educational experiences of Native students challenge our faculty as they approach issues of academic standards, assessment and inclusiveness. Non-Native faculty, in particular, recognize that they are "outsiders" with limited access to resources and experiences and that they must rely on their NWIC colleagues and community partners to give them practical access to community knowledge.

Students reiterate preference for the hiring of Native faculty in order to put a Native "face" on their education. We noted that students sometimes identify culture at NWIC as a surface experience such as basket-making and are often unable to name the cultural integration occurring in their courses. Student perceptions of what is cultural integration are a concern for NWIC faculty and administrators.

Students appear to also not be aware of their own prior cultural knowledge and how it serves their educational experience.

NWIC's institutional assessment process is designed to respond to issues of cultural knowledge through the cultural outcomes and their related evaluative instruments and strategies. Instructors develop rubrics that describe effective cultural outcomes as part of the overall course assessment. In addition, the college is moving definitively toward the use of portfolios and demonstrations as tools to aid in assessing cultural competencies.

NEXT STEPS AND RECOMMENDATIONS

Building a matrix describing the relationship between the Native scholar experiences supporting Native, place-based education and the non-Native scholar participating in the same was a result of this review of our experience. This matrix frames how these two critical components of a successful integration program can interact:

Native Scholar Experience Supporting Native, Place-Based Education	Non-Native Scholar Experience Supporting Native, Place-Based Education
Practical experience with fishing, aquaculture, resource management, governance, family systems	Prior experience with Native resource environments Prior experience such as the Peace Corps which exposes individuals to resource issues in diverse communities
Prior experience working with people of mainstream cultures (such as negotiation teams, advisory committees, employment)	Opportunity to have lived and worked with people of other cultures including other tribal cultures Comfort with being an "outsider"
Experience of colonization	Knowledge of colonization and understanding of its influences on institutional practices, society and individual experiences
Ability to identify topical subjects that can be used to integrate science and cultural knowledge such as: • Canoe pulling • Creation stories • Natural resources (land, water, air, plants, animals)	Ability to identify subject matter that can benefit from integrated knowledge such as: • Local flora and fauna as basis for place-based experiences • Critical tribal issues such as fishing, forest management, water
Participation in traditional cultural and spiritual opportunities for reflection	Self-reflection about relationship as a non-Native to the mission and the practice of willingness to serve institutional mission

Identification of the deliberate, exact relationship between the individual, the family, the land, environment and tribal history	Recognition that students have a connection to the land and environment deeply embedded in thousands of years of relationships
Establishment of a value in trusting relationships with non-Native faculty who teach in STEM and other areas through cultivation of relationships	Willingness to persevere in the development of trusting relationships

Recommendations

The following recommendations are applicable across the tribal college system and are particularly focused on the NWIC experience:

Institutional Climate

Northwest Indian College's leadership identified the importance of "marketing" the experience of cultural integration to students, faculty and community. Many individuals, especially students and community members, do not see a connection between what they are learning and experiencing and their tribal culture and are therefore unable to realize that they are participating in a culturally integrated learning experience. From an institutional perspective, we may have to deliberately name the cultural experience in order to ensure the building of connections among the personal, tribal, and institutional experiences. The practice of deliberate intention is grounded in cultural practices of tribal elders and traditional people. Two approaches for this could be (1) the implementation of cultural outcomes and (2) curriculum mapping that specifically focuses on restoration of knowledge that has been taken away through colonization.

At a tribal college there is an assumption that the approach of cultural integration should be and is institutionalized across all curricula and daily practice. This can be checked through examination of the content and implementation of the college's mission, strategic plan, institutional and program outcomes, course outcomes, and assessment which need to be linked through cultural practice and intention.

Assessment: Cultural Outcomes

A cultural institutional mission is not enough to create the classroom based integration necessary to a successful tribal education experience for students. Assessment strategies including institutional, program and course cultural outcomes combined with effective evaluative strategies strengthen the

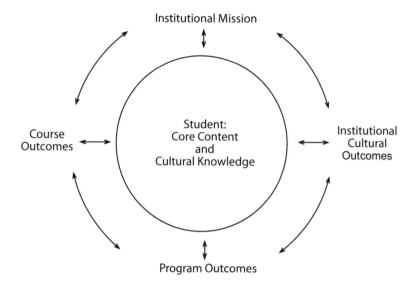

institution-wide approach to cultural integration and facilitate individual commitment. This circular relationship provides students with the best opportunity for Native knowledge to be part of their core educational experience.

The interrelatedness of all aspects of the student's education—the holistic approach—grounds faculty, staff, and institutional leaders in practices that are transferable across experiences, disciplines, and approaches to education. Participating with the student in an educational process that is holistic replicates the life experience of students which must, of necessity, be part of the whole tribal experience.

Faculty Development

As discussed earlier, deliberate approaches to the development of faculty cultural content knowledge and improving skills and abilities of faculty to teach culturally diverse students benefit the institution when conducted over an extended period of time. These strategies could include immersion experiences, presentations by speakers, videos, workshops, and conference participation. Evidence of improved instruction should be both observable and intentional. Evidence could come from surveys of teaching strategies, evidence-based review of syllabi, faculty evaluation and observation.

Training faculty on various strategies that facilitate dialogue such as Structured Controversy, Non-Violent Communication, Conversation-based Engagement, Deliberative Dialogue and various mediation, narrative or story-telling strategies can contribute to the ability of faculty to identify and foster integration experiences.

An understanding of assimilation and colonization and their impacts on people as well as a broad understanding of Native history contributes to improved abilities and participation with student learning. Role-playing and simulations, training by specialists in race relations and reconciliation, readings and media events, faculty discussions and exploration of materials and their experience and deeper exposure to community are strategies to aid this understanding.

Tribal colleges should also continue to deliberately develop the next generation of Native faculty and leaders who have core knowledge and deep bonding with their place and their people. This training of emerging faculty and leaders requires an institutional investment in both formal education and access to cultural resources.

Training for Cultural Resource People

Individuals who serve as cultural resources to STEM faculty benefit from exposure to educational methodologies and curriculum development skills. This helps them understand how information can be presented for easy access by faculty and creates stronger links between content knowledge and cultural knowledge.

Library and Instructional Resources

Dedicated effort is required for sufficient institutional resources to be devoted to acquisition of Native science and Native studies materials for individual faculty and student use. Annotated bibliographies are a useful tool for faculty especially if generated by Native resource people knowledgeable of the requirements of cultural integration—subject matter, accessibility, integrity of the research and information, and appropriateness relative to institutional course requirements.

Northwest Indian College has an annotated bibliography of the Lummi people as part of a Coast Salish bibliography developed by the Coast Salish Institute. This bibliography is available through the Institute.

Through the support of the Northwest Area Foundation, NWIC developed a *Traditional Tribal Leadership* training curriculum that is adaptable as courses, for lessons, and in workshop and community education formats. This curriculum focuses on traditional tribal understanding of leadership, fosters self-reflection and guides the participant toward the practice of leadership that is based in knowledge of inherent identity, relationships and cultural traditions. This curriculum can also serve as a model of cultural integration for faculty.

CONCLUSION

In *Power and Place: Indian Education In America,* written with Daniel Wildcat (Fulcrum Publishing, 2001), the late Vine Deloria, Jr. wrote:

> Education in the traditional setting occurs by examples and not as a process of indoctrination. That is to say, elders are the best living examples of what the end product of education and life experiences should be. We sometimes forget that life is exceedingly hard and that none of us accomplishes everything we could possibly do or even many of the things we intended to do.

Cultural integration at Northwest Indian College is an on-going process grounded in a long history of practice by both Native and non-Native faculty and strengthened by the commitment of the institutional leadership and community to tribal identity for students. Our mission, "Through education, Northwest Indian College promotes indigenous self-determination and knowledge," guides our efforts.

Cheryl Crazy Bull is president of Northwest Indian College in Bellingham, Washington. She wishes to thank all NWIC faculty and students who contributed ideas for the content of this chapter, including:

Sharon Kinley, Director, Coast Salish Institute

John Rombold, Science Faculty

Ted Williams, Academic Programs Coordinator

Indians Can Do Math

Carol Bowen

For many years, Haskell Indian Nations University offered what was essentially a community college mathematics program. It consisted of a couple of service courses, college algebra, and a large remedial program ranging from basic arithmetic through the equivalent of Algebra II even as the university was moving towards baccalaureate degrees. Our department was far behind the rest of the university. With the help of a National Science Foundation Tribal Colleges and Universities Program (TCUP) grant and a National Institutes of Health RISE grant, we reorganized our programs. We did not want to slight the remedial program, but we needed to develop and offer the core courses for math-dependent degrees.

The RISE grant supports computer assisted instruction for prealgebra, beginning algebra, and intermediate algebra. This provided the faculty time to develop a core calculus and analytic geometry sequence. We are under no illusion that our students can just walk into a course. We spend a lot of time planning topics and placing students throughout the sequence, keeping in mind that we try to accomplish in a semester what takes a year in high school. That's not easy for the faculty or the students.

Over time, I have developed a repertoire of techniques—some that have worked, and some that have not. I suspect this is true of most tribal college faculty. We should share our approaches with mainstream schools. We really are quite accomplished and dynamic. For example, a few of us at Haskell have developed an atypical approach to course design. Instead of a straight lecture and lab scenario, we offer an action packed hands-on course. This works well with lab courses. The students respond and retain more information.

I have not figured out how to implement this strategy in a standard math course, however. The dilemma is always how do you allow students time to discover a concept while maintaining the rigor of the course? I have heard more than once that students in other countries cover fewer topics but in greater depth. I wish I knew what those topics were! I am very cautious and try to cover the standard stuff, since our students will transfer to other schools. Depth is a problem.

Major Movements in the Teaching
of College Mathematics

There were three major movements in the teaching of college mathematics that influenced my teaching—research by Uri Triesman, the Harvard Consortium, and constructivist learning. Each of these movements had strategies that I hope make my teaching of mathematics more effective. Triesman challenged minority students rather than remediate them, Harvard made mathematics an experience, and constructivist learning is hands-on.

During the 1980s, Uri Treisman, a member of the faculty at The University of California-Berkley, wondered why many Asian students excelled in calculus courses while African American students had disproportionately high failure rates even though the two groups had comparable S.A.T. scores in high school. He found that the African American students tended to study alone and separated their academic work from their social lives. In contrast, Asian students integrated their intellectual and social lives by creating academically focused social groups. From this, Treisman devised an educational model that stressed collaborative teaching/learning strategies rather than isolated learning, using challenging problems rather than procedural applications of formulas, and enticing students to use what they knew. The result was significantly higher grades and completion rates for African American students. The model has been widely replicated nationwide.

It sounds great: Students work in groups, combining their knowledge and skills to approach a sophisticated problem. We are not talking about worksheets of practice problems, but an in-depth challenge. But while I occasionally do this in my classes, I don't think I could sustain such an effort for an entire semester. Once the students are grouped, the instructor faces a few challenges: 1) students are not accustomed to creative efforts; 2) students are hesitant to engage in creative efforts; and 3) students do not know how to interact creatively. By the time students reach the college level, they are pretty much conditioned to sit, listen, and do what they are told (or not). Even though their cultural upbringing would suggest that Native students think differently, they try to fit in.

The "do-what-you're-told" conditioning is very strong. Students will tell me there is only one proper way to solve a problem. It takes them about six weeks to believe that I really do know a little math, and that there is more to math than providing answers. One of my colleagues talks about students who have difficulty moving from concrete to abstract reasoning. The creativity, the ability to analyze, is just not there after so many years of doing things in a very structured way.

The Harvard Calculus Consortium

In the late 1980s, there was a major movement out of Harvard University to change the approach to teaching calculus and other STEM math courses by what was called The Calculus Consortium (Hughes-Hallet et al). The premise was that students were not developing the flexibility and creativity to really use the mathematics they had learned. "Conceptual" and "modeling" approaches replaced plug-n-chug and stamina. Using the "rule of four" (present topics geometrically, numerically, analytically, and verbally) works well. I use it at every level on a daily basis. Doesn't this sound like a holistic approach? The Harvard approach borrows the concept of group work from Uri Triesman. The entire text, which was funded by NSF, has challenging but do-able problems.

Constructivist Learning

There is much to learn from the theory of constructivist learning (Selden). Unlike discovery learning, constructive learning uses problem driven concepts. Letting a problem drive a lesson encourages students to build on what they already know. Building on what a student already knows is just good teaching.

Here's how constructivist learning can be integrated into a course. First, make a list of all the concepts you want to cover in a course. Then create a class exercise that uses a few of the most elementary topics. The next exercise will include the elementary topics covered and a few new topics. Check them off the list as you progress through the semester.

COURSE SYLLABUS Concepts: A, B, C, D, E, F, G, H, I	
Class Session #1	A
Class Session #2	A, B
Class Session #3	A, C
Class Session #4	A, B, C
Class Session #5	A, B, D
Class Session #6	A, B, C, D
Class Session #7	B, F, G
Class Session #8	C, E, H
Class Session #9	G, H, I
Exam	A through I

All class sessions are held in a lab setting. Lectures are short introductions to the day's challenge. After a couple of sessions, the students will start working together, and sharing ideas and debating the validity of their strategies. Often, they stay after class because they are not willing to break their concentration.

Questions are asked on a need to know basis. The questions will go beyond what you would have asked in a controlled classroom setting.

Haskell's Computer Applications Lab is arranged to accommodate constructivist learning. The computers are arranged around the perimeter of the room so that the instructor can see the screens and interact individually with students. The center of the room has tables for books, notes, and discussions. The students are encouraged to work together, sharing and collaborating.

We developed a relationship with the University of Kansas for GIS instruction. KU's geography department needed a graduate position, and we needed part-time instruction. This has been a very successful arrangement for both institutions. Doctoral students get an opportunity to teach and otherwise interact with students while being mentored. We get top-notch geography/GIS knowledge for the classroom. The course is taught using constructivist learning in the lab. The first half of the course is devoted to developing skills. In the second half of the course, students learn to use those skills and develop individual projects as part of their final grades. Invariably, a new KU instructor will want to change the course to a lecture/lab structure. It takes about six weeks for him or her to adapt. I have heard from the instructors who have moved on that they have rearranged their labs like ours, and will teach no other way.

Favorite Strategies

Hands in Your Pockets

Teaching is most effective when the strategies are comfortable for both the instructor and the students. Have no pride. Borrow strategies from anywhere. One of my favorites comes from training in Total Quality Management (TQM). TQM is a business management strategy (Peter Drucker). The training was for faculty and staff at Haskell. It's the brainstorming session that I use most. Instead of taking a math problem through to its conclusion, I ask the students to put their hands in their pockets and give me some guesses (hopefully educated, but not always). I write them on the board out of the way and label them "estimates." When we get close to the end, I ask them to finish up and let me know their results. It takes a while, but I can usually get half a dozen responses, none of which agree. As the students watch the proposed answers go up, they will withdraw their answers if they realize their answer is wrong and can tell me why. For example, "Oh, I had my calculator in degree mode." Once everyone agrees on the answer, we compare the result to the estimates. Like in TQM, the input of each member of the class (team) is important and can lead to a collective, reasonable result. The strategy also emphasizes a workplace skill. Only in the classroom can one work in total isolation.

Verbalize

Students should have a good number sense—a feel for the problem they are working on *at any course level!* With a sketch or some approximations, have the students take time to speculate on a solution and describe a strategy. Forget the rules. Let it be casual.

Consider the following:

π is approximately 3.14,
e is approximately 2.7. Estimate π/*e*.

Round off π and *e* to the nearest whole number. And?
Yes, they both round off to 3. Then, π/*e* ≈ 3/3 which is 1.

So, π/*e* is a smidgeon more than one, and *e*/π is a smidgeon less than one. Try the following with your hands in your pockets:

Simplify: $\frac{\pi}{e} + \frac{e}{\pi}$. Estimate: $1^+ + 1^- \approx 2$. Verbally: A smidgeon more than one plus a smidgeon less than one is about 2.

Those of us who grew up with slide rules and Chemical Rubber Company (CRC) handbooks have an advantage.[1] We knew how to estimate, interpolate, extrapolate, and consequently anticipate. We learned how to use semi-log, log, loglog, and polar graph paper. It's not the same when a number pops up on a calculator. We have deprived our students of number sense. They will sacrifice the accuracy of a fraction for the calculator readiness of a decimal. To compensate for this deficiency in trig functions, I like to demonstrate how the trig function values relate to each other using a spreadsheet.

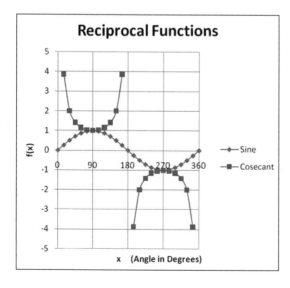

Degree	Sine	Cosecant
0	0	
15	0.258819	3.863703
30	0.5	2
45	0.707107	1.414214
60	0.866025	1.154701
75	0.965926	1.035276
90	1	1
105	0.965926	1.035276
120	0.866025	1.154701
135	0.707107	1.414214
150	0.5	2
165	0.258819	3.863703
180	1.23E-16	
195	-0.25882	-3.8637
210	-0.5	-2
225	-0.70711	-1.41421
240	-0.86603	-1.1547
255	-0.96593	-1.03528
270	-1	-1
285	-0.96593	-1.03528
300	-0.86603	-1.1547
315	-0.70711	-1.41421
330	-0.5	-2
345	-0.25882	-3.8637
360	-2.5E-16	

Suggested questions:

Why is there no value for the Cosecant at $x = 0$ degrees?
(Ans. Csc = 1/sin $\rightarrow$ 1/0 which is undefined.) What do the Sine
and Cosecant have in common? (Ans. Both are equal to one
at odd multiples of 90 degrees.) Why is sin(180) = 1.23E - 16?
(Ans. Calculators give round off errors. The sin(180) is actually 0.
Calculators and computers do not give exact answers. See graph.)

Students appreciate the development of a trig table before their very eyes. They will ask for a printout to use for reference. Note that when you set up the spreadsheet, you will get bizarre values and the graph looks goofy (see the original table and graph below). If you are quick enough with a spreadsheet, the students can watch while you adjust the values. This is a great opportunity to discuss the use of calculators and computers, limits of a function, and other topics that are difficult to explain otherwise. The previous graph is an adjusted graph.

Degree	Sine	Cosecant
0	0	#DIV/0!
15	0.258819	3.863703
30	0.5	2
45	0.707107	1.414214
60	0.866025	1.154701
75	0.965926	1.035276
90	1	1
105	0.965926	1.035276
120	0.866025	1.154701
135	0.707107	1.414214
150	0.5	2
165	0.258819	3.863703
180	1.23E-16	8.16E+15

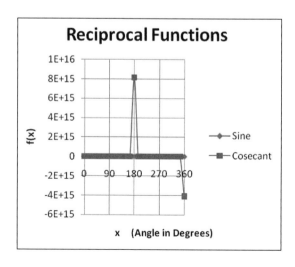

A spreadsheet can also help relate a graph to the x-y values. Below is a set of ordered pairs with an accompanying graph. Students can compare the numbers to the graph for a better understanding of how they are related. Oops. Did I make an error?

X	Y
-4.0	13.0
-3.5	9.3
-3.0	6.0
-2.5	3.3
-2.0	1.0
-1.5	-0.8
-1.0	-2.0
-0.5	-2.8
0.0	-3.0
0.5	-2.8
1.0	-2.0
1.5	-0.8
2.0	5.0
2.5	3.3
3.0	6.0
3.5	9.3
4.0	13.0

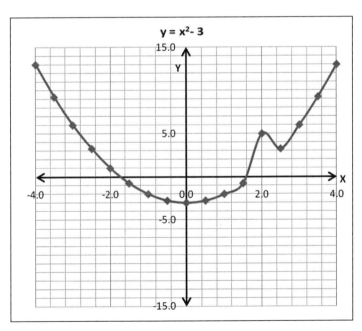

$$y = x^2 - 3$$

Negative numbers are funny. In the 1980s, many of our students arrived without any algebra in their backgrounds, so we offered Introduction to Algebra, which is roughly equivalent to the classic ninth grade algebra. One semester's class openly laughed at the concept of negative numbers. Another lesson learned. Math is not necessarily logical. It depends on your worldview.

On Geometry

Geometry is rather basic knowledge for any STEM student. Many Native students are at a disadvantage because they do not know geometry. Can you imagine doing a shadow problem with no knowledge of similar triangles? Sometimes, Native students aspiring to a STEM career do not even know how to use area and perimeter formulas of a plane figure. There are a lot of reasons why this happens. The bottom line is that we have to try to cover basic geometry topics like the area of a triangle or trapezoid and Euclidean geometry on the fly.

Geometry is typically not taught in college. If a student does not take geometry in high school, he or she has missed an opportunity. We tried to offer a geometry course at Haskell. Enrollment was low. Students managed to get through without it. However, STEM students have a hard time without the Euclidean geometry background of geometric relationships and proofs. Without geometry, trigonometry is difficult to learn. Haskell's Math Department has incorporated an overview at the beginning of the trigonometry course with some success, but there is little time to explore the relationships and intricacies of lines and angles. It is amazing how many students have earned STEM degrees with this handicap. I don't think I could have done it.

Geoboard

A geoboard can make quick work of explaining why the area of a triangle is $A = \frac{1}{2}bh$ or why the area of a parallelogram is $A = bh$ just like a rectangle. Geoboards can be purchased, but they are easy to make. Mine is a scrap of ¼ inch plywood with ¾ inch brads for posts. I marked off 2 centimeter squares on a piece of old linen stationery, decoupaged it to the plywood, and nailed in the brads. Colored rubber bands make the shapes easy to see. Count the line segments around the edge of a shape for perimeter and count the squares for area.

The first step is to illustrate and discuss the area and perimeter of a rectangle. Then, add another rubber band to outline a triangle. The students will respond intuitively that the area is half the rectangle, but they will be unsure about the perimeter of the triangle. By arranging the rubber bands in different ways, you can use what they already know to explain other triangles, parallelograms and trapezoids. Circles would be a stretch. (Chuckle.)

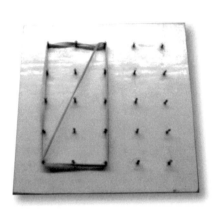 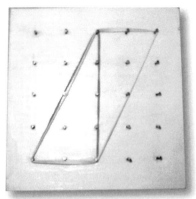

Basic Geometry

Purchasing wrapping paper for a gift lends itself to a plane/solid geometry problem that can be approached several ways with different sets of skills. Students are quite creative in their approaches. The problem goes like this: Given a gift box with dimensions 10 x 14 x 4 inches high and a package of wrapping paper with two sheets, each 20 inches by 2 feet, can you wrap the box with one sheet? (No joke. I got those wrapping paper dimensions off a package in a local store.) Students will try calculating surface area, but soon realize that the usual plug-n-chug approach will not work. So they get more creative. One student simulated the problem with a homemade box and newspaper cut to dimension; another student visualized the box flattened. I noticed that the same local store now has a kit with *three* boxes and wrapping paper provided. I can hardly wait until next Christmas.

 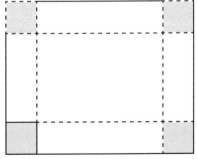

Test Generators

I've been experimenting with publisher-provided test generators. My original motivation was the department testing and assessment measures we have been working on. Test generators are convenient, and they definitely cover the material from the text. It's easy to create multiple choice exams that are more manageable at the department level. The downside is the rigidity and plug-n-chug nature of a generated test. The questions are organized by the sections and topics in the text. There will be a handful of almost identical problems for a topic like "Use completing the square to solve the quadratic equation." The concepts in a chapter are never pulled together to apply to a new situation. If you have more than one faculty member using the same test generator, all of the questions will be out there very soon. As I became more familiar with the test generators, I noticed that each of them had advantages that I had not fully explored. The graphics capabilities are very good, although not common to all. Some of the graphics can be saved as .jpg and used in other software.

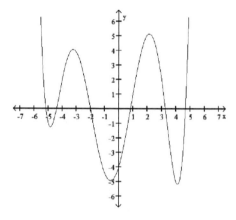

At first, I avoided testbank editor options. Looked like trouble. This semester, I am gradually including a few of my own problems to the database for each exam, so that I will have more problems to choose from and more original problems.

Interest

In every course, we have application problems involving interest, yet we never take the time to explain what interest is. This forces a student to use "plug-n-chug" without understanding the application. In College Algebra, for example, students are introduced to simple interest, compound interest, and continuously compounded interest. In Table 1, simple interest is used repeatedly to demonstrate how the cost of a loan accumulates. The class was divided into two groups, bankers and borrowers. The borrowers are assigned to finance the purchase of their dream car. The lenders must bring in enough money to pay their salaries. It doesn't take long for the lenders to discover that they have to be competitive, and the borrowers will try to keep the cost of the loan down. All calculations are done by hand for each month. The lesson can be shortened by offering the current market rate for new cars. Some classes have derived the formula for compound interest.

Table 1: Simple Interest I-PRT

Loan amount: $ 25,000.00	Downpayment: $ 2,000.00			
Month Payment: $400.00	Rate: 8%			

Month	Payment	Paid Principle	Paid Interest	Balance Due
0	$	$	$	$ 23,000.00
1	$ 400.00	$ 246.67	$ 153.33	$ 22,753.33
2	$ 400.00	$ 248.31	$ 151.69	$ 22,505.02
3	$ 400.00	$ 249.97	$ 150.03	$ 22,255.06
4	$ 400.00	$ 251.63	$ 148.37	$ 22,003.42
TOTAL:			**$ 603.42**	

Purchasing a dream car is fun. The follow-up discussion on loans that students are familiar with—student loans, credit cards, pay-day loans, and so on—brings the point home. The Excel spreadsheet, Table 1, has built-in formulas so that students can try what-if scenarios.

Later in the course, in the exponential functions discussion, parallel examples of brute force by month (simple interest), using the compound interest formula, and the new continuously compounded interest formula illustrate an overview of the topic. During the 2008-2009 school year, because of the turbulent economy, we were able to expand the discussion and interpret the news. The students were motivated to develop their own strategies for surviving the economic crisis. Textbooks consistently avoid examples and problems involving loans, even though that is where the action is.

Simple Interest	Compound Interest	Continuously Compounded Interest
$I = PRT, A = P + I$	$A = P(1 + r/n)^{nt}$	$A = Pe^{rt}$

Problem of the Week

Haskell's Math Department has a whiteboard in the hall for the "Problem of the Week." Each correct solution is worth a lottery ticket. The problems are written to fit any level and are not tied to a specific course. At the end of the semester, a drawing is held for a prize. This semester, the prize was an iPod. The contest generated a lot of interest. Students would stand in front of the whiteboard to discuss the possibilities. This is a great place to enrich the students' backgrounds by using geometry, set theory, probability, networking, and so on. My suggestion is to call the "Problem of the Week" something else, because there were some weeks when we were fresh out of ideas or too busy to follow through. We actually do eight to ten problems a semester.

Circles

Tell me everything you know about a circle. Question: Why are circles important socially and culturally? Think about round dances, pow wow grounds, talking circles, round tables. This is a good time to introduce a locus of points definition. Use a cord and chalk to draw a circle on the board. (Board compasses are distracting. A simple 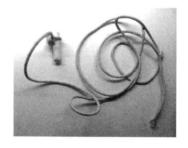 cord emphasizes the simple circle.) Students will usually start with the radius and diameter. Some will remember the area and circumference formulas.

Question: Why do a wristwatch and a wall clock give you the same information?

At the precalculus level, the discussion will lead to degree and radian measure with a clear understanding of the difference.

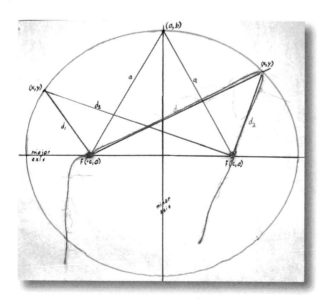

Conic sections

Developing conic sections from scratch gives student an understanding of formulas and proof that they cannot gain otherwise. Rather than trying to memorize the formulas, and perhaps the derivations, students have the opportunity to develop a style of notation and create labels and statements they need. Since the derivations rely heavily on the Pythagorean theorem, most students have all the knowledge they need. Focus on the ellipse. The picture at left shows flipchart paper tacked to a bulletin board. Use twine and colored chalk. After they have developed the formula for the ellipse and understand all its parts, the circle, parabola, and hyperbola logically follow.

Word Problems

If you want to scare the bejeebies out of someone, type up a paragraph from a romance novel and hand it to them. Tell them to solve the word problem. It could be a love triangle or a steamy affair, but the seemingly strong and intelligent reader will tremble with fear. They will not be able to read the paragraph. It's the "Grit your teeth and do it" approach we use. In the spirit of Uri Triesman, the Harvard Calculus Consortium, and constructivist learning, try something like the following.

> Imagine a main street in a pleasant town. There's a row of storefronts and a bank on one side of the street. On the other side of the street is a river with a boat dock. The river is flowing quietly at about 5 mph. Some guy robs the bank and takes off downstream in a waiting motorboat! The top speed for a motorboat in still water is 35 mph. The cops are standing on the shore, helpless, beside their cars. Then, 10 minutes later, an unsuspecting tourist docks a rented speed boat. Lieutenant (Student name here) flashes her/his badge and jumps into the speedboat to pursue the crook. The speedboat can travel 50 mph in still water.

Questions:

How fast is the motorboat traveling? (Ans. 40 mph)

Can the cop overtake the crook? How far from the dock? (Ans. Yes. 24.5 mi)

Draw a sketch of the pursuit.

If the cop can catch up to the motorboat, how long will it take? (Ans. 26.6 min)

Are there any technicalities to consider? (units—minutes vs. hours)

What if the crook had taken off upstream? What would change?

Why would the crook head upstream? (Could be a waterfall downstream.)

I suppose a naturalist could reword this problem for animal predators and prey. I'm from Chicago. This is what I know. These problems take more time, but more students will comprehend the concepts. The presentation has more depth. It's quality time.

Email Promotes Written Communication

I pulled the quote below from *Long Son* (Bowen). The lead character, DuPre is Métis. The story takes place in Montana. I usually send this out in email for extra credit and require an email response. It's a nice inequality problem. Students like to use email. Some of them will text from their phones. Email is a good communication tool. The user is forced to rely on the written word.

> "It was early afternoon. He and Jacqueline had left right after Raymond had been taken out in the helicopter. It was a six- or seven-hour drive from Cooper to Billings at sixty-five. Du Pre made it in four hours." (Bowen)

1. How far is it from Cooper to Billings? (Ans. $390 < d < 455$ mi)
2. How fast did Du Pre drive? (Ans. $97.5 < r < 113.75$ mph)

Indians Can't Do Math!

I hear all the time that Indians can't do math. Accepting this kind of conditioning makes Indian people dependent on others. What about self determination? Mathematics is strength. Tribes need math to determine and manage budgets, interpret reports, author reports, make policy decisions, manage resources, assess environmental quality, even to determine allotments. Math is power. For example, tribes contract with outsiders to collect and report data to the federal government, not knowing if they got their money's worth. And, sadly, some of the tribes do not even want a copy of the data for their own use. Which is worse—that they had to hire someone to collect the data, that they could easily be scammed, or that they do not use the data for their own benefit?

The Negative Mantra

Math avoidance is very strong among Indian students. Students with high math scores often downplay their ability by getting low grades in math classes. Recently I helped a new student who had a decent score but who gave me the usual "I'm no good at math" line. I am not sure if he was trying to convince me or his fellow students, who were within earshot.

We should say to students who too readily confess that they cannot do math that such a statement makes for a self-fulfilling prophecy. It negates any innate capability they have and sets up a poor role model for nieces, nephews, siblings, and their own children. After hearing that negative mantra for so long, it takes incredible effort to resist the conditioning. And repeating the mantra multiplies the effect exponentially (uh-oh, math again). Is this a trend among Indian students or a national trend?

Opinion and Style Are In

Our entire nation is suffering from the belief that math is incomprehensible to the common person. This lazy thinking allows people to avoid critical analysis. It also leaves them vulnerable to twisted analysis and inaccurate conclusions. They accept statements made by people who sound authoritative. When readers, listeners and presenters all believe these conclusions, the facts are left behind and anyone who has number sense is at best ignored and at worst...well, let's not go there.

But the end result is that priorities and actions are based on opinion and style rather than logic and data. It's easy to find examples of words versus numbers. In a single newspaper, I found several, but the quote below was the shortest:

> Topeka—Several House members Thursday questioned whether any Kansan earned as little as the state minimum wage of $2.65 per hour.
>
> During a hearing on a bill to increase the state minimum wage, state Rep. Scott Schwab, R-Olathe, noted no one getting paid that amount testified to the committee.
>
> Schwab said he would pay anyone making the state minimum wage their lost wages and mileage to take time off from work and talk to the House Commerce and Labor Committee. (Rothschild)

It's hard to read a newspaper without wondering, "Do people really believe this stuff?" Could anyone making $2.65 an hour afford a car to drive to Topeka? That's $106 per week, or $5,512 a year assuming that the person has a full time job with holiday pay. Why would anyone rely on such testimony to establish that some workers are making $2.65 per hour? Shouldn't actual data carry more weight? Representative Schwab was trying to discredit words by suggesting that a more convincing argument than his own could not be found. Given that this debate has gone on for a few years, he may be right even though he may be wrong.

Here's a quote from one of my college algebra students,

> It is true most people don't know what they're reading about in newspapers; most people just ignore the real numbers and assume

that the numbers that are written down are the correct ones. I myself have come across numbers while I read an article or any type of paper and sometimes ignored numbers.

Relevance

Mathematics teachers constantly hear the challenge that we should make math more relevant. Given that we see the students three to five hours per week, the chance that we can turn the tide alone is pretty slim.

Let's take this thought a bit further. *Mathematics is not relevant if it is not used in other courses.* Why isn't the Mayan number system taught in a history course? Is there still math in sociology? How much math is actually used in environmental science? What's happening in education or politics? Name an academic discipline that does not relate to math.

Art?—Ratio and proportion, Fibonacci sequence.

Music?—fundamental frequency and harmonics, measuring the beat (fractions!).

Literature and philosophy?—Has anyone read *Cuckoo's Egg* or *Silicon Snake Oil*? (Stoll) How about *Through the Looking Glass?* (Carroll) or *The DaVinci Code*? (Brown)

History?—In some cultures, the struggle between numerology and numeracy complicated religion and politics. Mathematics was not always the structured discipline we know today.[2] It was downright dangerous.

There are several liberal arts math courses available now. Wouldn't it be interesting to start with an art course, and then branch off into math and science? Add a little philosophy and religion. That's how math and science began anyway.

Student Skills

There is no reason why our students would have the personal skills necessary to be successful in college. For a new student, the first six weeks of the semester are crucial. Orientation classes acclimate the students to the campus environment, introduce study technique, note-taking, and test-taking skills, and discuss time management. It is up to us, as instructors, to follow through on that message. We should talk to them about taking notes, keeping them organized, and using them. For example, we can break down the learning process into three stages: 1) Relate a new concept to something the students already know; 2) Develop an understanding of the concept; and 3) Teach them how and what to memorize so that they can move on to something new. If we do not teach student skills, we will lose students who could have been successful.

A good exam evaluates the students' ability to apply a combination of techniques and facts to new situations. We are misleading the students if we write an entire exam that merely tests one skill after the other. Would we expect an English instructor to test grammar skills and never test composition? Sometimes we do resort to skills tests as a matter of survival. It's difficult to reach out to the next cognitive level, but we are talking about college. We are talking about STEM fields.

Know Your Students

Each student has individual experiences that distinguish him or her from fellow students. Some will come to Haskell to learn what they can and go back home to help their tribes. Others do not want to go back to their tribe. Some know nothing about their tribes. Some have a traditional upbringing, but not all. *Do not assume you know your students' goals or their backgrounds.*

Young People Have Young Ideas

Back in the formative days for Web sites, there were distinct differences between the design ideas of Haskell's older faculty and staff and the younger high-tech students. The faculty and staff wanted a Web site full of history. The students were fine with the history, but wanted a more modern appearance. *We cannot presume to know what will appeal to students.*

Native Students Have Knowledge

The best way to teach students is to find out what they already know. You then have a foundation to build on. Native students may or may not know the standard stuff, but many of them have more life experience than mainstream students. I met a student this semester who had dropped out of school, moved around for a few years, and then decided to try college. He was one of the wisest students I have ever met. During enrollment, he talked to me about his goals. He took a long route to college, but he definitely has a plan now. All the jobs, financial experiences, and family contribute to his knowledge base.

Teach the Total Person

Native students have priorities that extend beyond education to family, jobs, and cultural beliefs and responsibilities. If a student's grandmother is very ill or they must participate in a ceremony, mathematics is not important. Nor is mathe-

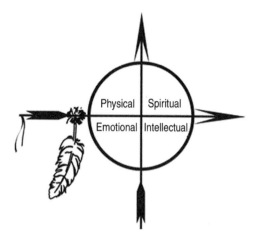

matics important if the student is trying to figure out how to pay rent. Help the students identify their goals and their options.

Observations From the Outside

There are less than twenty Native Americans with PhD's in mathematics. Consequently, the overwhelming task of incorporating Native cultures into mathematics defaults to non-Natives more often than not. There are some general philosophies that I think would benefit Native students while we are waiting for the next generation of Native PhD's in mathematics.

I do not have a Native cultural background. I have tried to identify topics and strategies that pique students' interests knowing full well that the students do not all have the same life experiences. Mathematics is going through a long overdue renaissance. There are so many current and relevant applications of mathematics; the discipline is really quite exciting.

Native Ways of Knowing

This is a difficult concept for me. I have read articles about Native ways of knowing and I have heard people speak of it, but the articles were not written by mathematicians and the speakers were not mathematicians. I am reminded of an AISES conference back in the 1980s. Vine Deloria was the keynote speaker. Deloria's theme was "just give me the information. I'll decide what to do with it." While Deloria was not a mathematician, that philosophy is far more honest than me trying to be something I am not. At the same time, I caution all instructors to remain open to new ideas. We should teach students wherever they come from and wherever they are going to. Bad grammar intended.

Carol Bowen has served on the faculty at Haskell Indian Nations University in mathematics since 1983. She is responsible for the development and operation of Haskell's lab for computer applications including GIS. She is currently coPI on an NSF TCUP grant, "Mathematics: Keystone for Success" and a partner in the NSF STC grant, Center for the Remote Sensing of Ice Sheets (CReSIS). Throughout her career, she has focused on interdisciplinary approaches and applied technologies related to mathematics.

ENDNOTES

1. CRC handbooks had math tables similar to the tables above. They were used before handheld calculators.
2. Come to think of it, mathematics is still complicating religion and politics.

REFERENCES

Bowen, Peter. *Long Son.* New York: St. Martin's Minotaur, 1999.

Brown, Dan. *The Da Vinci Code.* New York: Doubleday, 2003.

Carroll, Lewis. *Through the Looking Glass.* New York: Macmillan, 1871.

ExamView Test Generator, Version 5.1.1. FSCreations, Inc. 1999-2006.

"Galileo Galilei." *Wikipedia.* Web. 10 Jan. 2009.

Livio, Mario. *The Golden Ratio: The Story of PHI, the World's Most Astonishing Number.* New York: Broadway Books, 2002.

"Peter Drucker." *Wikipedia.* Web. 12 January 2009.

Posamentier, Alfred S., and Ingmar Lehmann. *A Biography of the World's Most Mysterious Number.* Amherst, New York: Prometheus, 2004.

Rothschild, Scott. "Wage proposal debated." *Lawrence Jounal-World* 6 March 2009: 3A.

Schmidt, Stanley. "Life of Fred." *Books from Fractions through Calculus and Statistics.* Polka Dot Publishing, n.d.

Seife, Charles. *Zero: The Biography of a Dangerous Idea.* New York: Penguin, 2005.

Selden, Annie and John. "Research Sampler Column, Constructivism." *MAA Online, The Mathematical Association of America.* Web. 14 January 2009.

Smith, Richard Manning. *Mastering Mathematics: How to Be a Great Math Student.* Florence, KY: Brooks Cole, 1999.

Stoll, Clifford. *The Cuckoo's Egg: Tracking a Spy Through the Maze of Computer Espionage.* New York: Pocket Books, 1990.

Test Generator and Testbank Editor, Version 7.3. Pearson Education, Tamarack Software, Inc. 1997-2005.

"Treisman's Model." *Merit Workshop program for Emerging Scholars in Mathematics.* Web. 12 January 2009.

TEACHING SUSTAINABILITY:

THE ROLE OF MATH AND SCIENCE AT COLLEGE OF MENOMINEE NATION

Marjane Ambler

For the Menominee people, culture hinges on sustainability. It is the key to their spirituality, language, and history. College of Menominee Nation (CMN) officials believe that sustainability is also key to their future—and to the future of the planet. They have found that students are naturally attracted to the college's activist role in slowing global warming. The students, too, want to make a difference.

Menominee culture and tradition teach never to take more resources than are produced within natural cycles. In the 1850s, Chief Oshkosh spoke against the prevailing attitude of the time, which was clearing timber to create farmlands. He said the Menominee people instead should cut their timber in a way that would assure timber would always be ready to cut.

Many indigenous peoples have a tradition of stewardship and using natural resources wisely as part of their spiritual responsibility. But none, perhaps, label it as specifically as the Menominee, who call it sustainable development.

Today, satellite images from outer space clearly show the boundaries of the Menominee Reservation in Wisconsin—timber on the inside and none on the outside. Over the last 150 years the Menominee have removed 2 billion board feet of lumber, but they have more timber available than when the reservation was created in 1854. People around the world recognize the Menominee for their sustainable forest.

This long history of sustainability offers several advantages to the tribal college in its efforts to fulfill its cultural mission. CMN can reach articulation agreements with other institutions that recognize sustainable development as a transferable credit. Sustainability principles can be taught to students of different tribes. Non-Indian faculty can be experts in sustainability while it might be more difficult and not always acceptable for non-tribal members to learn and then teach the local language, spirituality, or some traditional art form such as beading or basketry.

Interns and Sustainability Indicators Research

In 1993, the Menominee Nation chartered the College of Menominee Nation. The Menominee Reservation is located in east-central Wisconsin near Lake Michigan. The main campus is located on ten acres of the reservation in Keshena, Wisconsin. The college now has a second campus at Green Bay, Wisconsin, close to the Oneida Reservation. As a tribal college with an open enrollment policy, CMN serves mostly Menominee and Oneida students but also many non-Indian and other American Indian students. Accredited by the Higher Learning Commission of the North Central Association, CMN offers sixteen different associate degrees as well as three certificate programs. CMN has articulation agreements with eight colleges and universities.

In the same year, the visionary Menominee lawmakers also created a Sustainable Development Institute (SDI). The concept of sustainability was gaining currency then around the world. A year earlier in 1992 at Rio de Janeiro, Brazil, the United Nations had adopted a comprehensive plan for sustainability, especially in the management of forests.

The Menominee wanted SDI to devote itself to research, education, and outreach. Because these roles fit naturally into the college mission, SDI later became a part of the tribal college, according to Melissa Cook (Menominee), one of the members of the advisory board that helped establish SDI's vision and objectives. She is now the director of SDI.

As implemented by the College of Menominee Nation, sustainability encompasses much more than forests or even natural resources. The Menominee model is holistic, including six dimensions: natural environment, land and sovereignty, institutions, technology and science, economics, and human/ culture.

In March 2007 College of Menominee Nation President S. Verna Fowler, Ph.D., (Menominee/ Stockbridge-Munsee) was one of the first signatories to the American College and University Presidents Commitment to Climate Change. She also participates in conferences of the Clinton Global Initiative. When Fowler has spoken to former President Bill Clinton and to other college presidents at national conferences, she has emphasized her holistic vision and the importance of going beyond the agenda that most of them have set for themselves, focusing on energy, recycling, and climate.

By signing the commitment, the colleges and universities agreed to conduct a comprehensive greenhouse gas emissions inventory, develop an institutional action plan for becoming climate neutral, and initiate two tangible actions to reduce greenhouse gas emissions. The CMN Sustainable Development Institute, naturally, broadened that mission. It hired a sustainability coordinator in 2008 to lead a research project documenting the college's sustainability indicators. The coordinator, Beau Mitchell (Chippewa Cree of Rocky Boy), is creating a template for use by other tribal colleges and universities (TCUs). Mitchell presented his indicators project to the American Indian Higher Education Consortium in March 2009 in Missoula, Montana.

This research project—as with about 75 percent of the research projects at SDI—involves students. Although CMN is a two-year institution, tribal college staff members see many advantages to teaching students research skills. The internship experience demonstrates tangible, real-life applications that make their course work more meaningful. This encourages their thirst for knowledge, and most go on to get their four-year degrees, according to Mike Dockry, the USDA Forest Service liaison to the Sustainable Development Institute. The internships also help prepare global citizens, who understand the importance of sustainability. SDI benefits, too, according to Melissa Cook. "Native students come with a wealth of knowledge."

The college turned to students as well as staff and faculty to brainstorm about what a sustainable college might look like. Suggestions ranged from healthier food choices to harnessing more alternative energy sources. After the visioning sessions, the college staff agreed upon a set of sustainability indicators that includes not only typical data such as energy efficiency but others such as culture and health. The assumption is that an unhealthy person cannot be expected to recycle, for example.

Intern Menomin Hawpetoss helped with the greenhouse gas inventory at CMN. She designed, distributed, and collected surveys to benchmark the commuter habits of the CMN students, staff, and faculty and created a database with the results. Mitchell said such data is important if they want to become a carbon neutral campus. The resulting document will also be educational, explaining what greenhouse gases are and how they are generated.

Student intern Jeremy Wescott assisted with collecting data for the U.S. Environmental Protection Agency's Energy Star Benchmarking and inputting the data into a spreadsheet and into Energy Star's Benchmarking Web site. He also assisted with writing the Tribal Green Resource Guide for the *Tribal College Journal* (Vol. 20, No. 2, Winter 2008). Another student intern is assisting Mitchell with analyzing waste streams—going through all the trash generated at the college.

In spring 2009, the college hired student interns/ research assistants to interview tribal elders for the sustainable indicators project. Mitchell said they would ask the elders how they feel about trees and water, for example, and to share their stories. Mitchell said this will get youth back in touch with their elders while collecting qualitative data about sustainability. It will also help perpetuate the oral cultural traditions.

Sustainable Curriculum

All students who attend College of Menominee Nation must take the Introduction to Sustainability course as a general education requirement. The requirement demonstrates the college's commitment to create global citizens who understand the importance of living sustainably and to thread the concept through the entire curriculum. For their final paper, students write about how sustainability pertains to their fields and how they would apply what they learned. Instructor William Van Lopik, Ph.D., said students have written papers about the applicability of sustainability principles to fields as diverse as domestic violence, nursing care, teaching third graders, designing clothes, and working in a casino.

Students often report back to Van Lopik about changes to their lifestyles. Several began recycling; one asked his employer to use less Styrofoam at the restaurant. "Students like to get involved in projects that they know are going to make a difference," Van Lopik said.

Patrick Waukau majored in business until he took the intro class. "It opened my eyes, and I figured I wanted to help people instead of working at a casino and perpetrating bad habits. That would be something you could feel good about." He completed his associate degree in sustainable development in 2008, and now he plans to get a bachelor's degree in environmental design at the University of Wisconsin-Green Bay.

Some of the other faculty members are beginning to integrate sustainability concepts into their curriculum. For example, students can use the same final paper for their English composition course and for the sustainable development introduction course. Business classes discuss green businesses and take field trips to recycling sites. The college has a new trades program—sustainable residential building.

As a result of the introductory class, Van Lopik said many students have changed their academic fields and are now enrolled in or have graduated from universities in relevant programs. The CMN Introduction to Sustainable Development course is accepted by all the other schools in the University of Wisconsin system, he said. At some institutions, it satisfies the requirement for environmental literacy. As sustainable development becomes more of a mainstream concept, more schools are integrating it into their curriculum.

For more than a decade the Menominee tribal college has been offering a two-year sustainable development associate degree program. Students who major in sustainable development take Implementing Sustainable Development. A recent class project was measuring the amount of recycled material gathered on campus through participation in the nationwide college contest, Recyclemania. CMN students have participated in Recyclemania for several years.

The college hopes to create its own four-year degree in sustainable development in the future, but for now the emphasis is on giving students the philosophical and practical grounding for careers in fields such as Geographic Information Systems, natural resources, planning, and community development. CMN graduates can design their own fields of study at the University of Wisconsin-Madison around sustainability, but most are going into established departments, according to Van Lopik.

Now the college is developing an associate degree program in Sustainable Forestry. Victoria Yazzie, Ph.D. (Diné) said the Sustainable Forestry Program has been approved by the curriculum committee, and in spring 2009, she was developing courses. Yazzie, who has a doctorate degree in forestry from the University of Montana, tells her students, "You can be scientists without giving up your tribal identity." Her students learn that tribes control a limited amount of resources; it is important for tribal natural resource managers to protect them for younger generations and to perpetuate the sustainability tradition.

Yazzie is a Diné from the Southwest and not a member of the local tribes served by the College of Menominee Nation. To indigenize the courses, Yazzie has invited professionals from the Menominee Tribal Enterprise to speak, such as a forest ecologist and a wildlife officer, both of whom are members of local tribes. The courses will use the Menominee Tribal Enterprise forest as a case study for technical courses, such as remote/ aerial sensing and Geographic Information Systems. To increase her own understanding, Yazzie is studying the Menominee language, history, and traditions with the help of tribal mentors.

Van Lopik, a non-Indian who has taught at the college for seven years, said he and his students have a symbiotic learning process—they learn together. After living in El Salvador for six years, he can share stories about the challenges faced by indigenous movements in other countries. He has taken CMN students to Chiapas, Mexico, where they have become inspired by coffee farmers and by women gathering newspaper off the streets, mixing it with flowers and herbs, and making their own paper.

Both Van Lopik and Yazzie bring in guest speakers from local tribes. The college also got a grant so that indigenous people from El Salvador and Guatemala could come to Wisconsin and teach advanced permaculture, underwriting the course for ten students to take it. "You can take Master Gardener classes anywhere, but it lacks the spiritual aspect that these people brought," he said.

The sustainability introductory class has clearly excited the imaginations of students. Van Lopik's teaching assistant, Dolores Cobb, majors in Sustainable Development. She received an award in 2009 at the Clinton Global Initiative annual conference for her efforts to implement permaculture concepts at the community level.

Van Lopik points with pride to students and alumni who are researching and practicing sustainability outside the classroom:

- Student Cheyenne Caldwell helped spearhead the Great Lakes Environmental Protection Agency E-Waste effort, in which Menominee area households dropped off televisions, radios, computers, and batteries.
- Sustainable Development major Luis Ortiz established his own corporation, which retrofits standard automobiles to run on water, a hydrogen fuel supplement.
- Studying about "Resource Rebels" in his Sustainable Development class inspired student Marcus Grignon to start a non-profit organization called Citizens for a Sustainable Future. He is interested in innovations such as motorized and electric conversion kits for bicycles, motorized bicycle and pedal bicycle highways, and hydrogen fuel cell transportation systems.
- Dan Hawk is making pyrogenic carbon from a furnace that he designed. He believes that it can be used for solid carbon sequestration and as a filter for toxic wastes at Superfund sites.
- Justin Gauthier is studying to be a certified vermiculturalist, using worms to compost.
- Ben Daniels had an internship with NASA, sponsored by the American Indian Higher Education Consortium, at the Goddard Space Flight Center. In 2006, he won an award from NASA for his research on "Global Warming and the Future of the Menominee Forest."

TECHNOLOGY CURRICULUM

In 2009, Nathan Fregien began teaching a new class on creating digital video, in addition to his Web design and graphic design classes. In the digital video class, students create a digital biography portraying who they are and how they see the world. When the student is Native, his or her project naturally expresses culture as well as conveying art. Fregien's students bring many aspects of their culture to class, such as beadwork, woodlands-style graphic drawing, nature photographs, and appliqué. They incorporate that into PowerPoint presentations and later, as they get more sophisticated, into film and different interactive screen environments.

"They capture their physical art in a digital format and then compose it on a digital canvas," he said. One student brought in handmade artwork and put it into the Flash application, creating an animation for interactive screen environments. Another student put an animated GIF file of himself and his rez car on MySpace.

"Students are using modern tools to reinvent culture and art in a way that is still respectful," he said. Students can express themselves and their identity in an inventive, interdisciplinary way. They learn hands-on about the increasingly important cultural artifacts that recorded media and digitized artwork produce. They also learn to think critically about the social, economic, ethical, and cultural effects of the emerging media. They learn different Web 2.0 technologies, digital imaging and scanning, video and audio mixing, web-based computer programming languages, and creative writing skills that amplify their messages. Fregien says the students' message is, "I am Native, and this is what I stand for."

The Sustainable Development Institute sponsored its first Sustainable Film Contest in spring 2009. Entrants were asked to make a three- to seven-minute film to "let the world know what sustainable and or climate change mean to you." Fregien said six people were submitting entries, two of whom were college students and one a high school student.

In his role as the multimedia technical coordinator for the Sustainable Development Institute, Fregien also works with the Menominee Culture and Language program. Since there are only a small number of people who can speak the language fluently, the tribe wants to use innovative tools to increase that number. Fregien and the language instructor are creating podcasts and other interactive learning tools, such as a learning DVD, using recordings of traditional Menominee speakers.

A non-Indian who graduated from the College of Menominee Nation in 2002, Fregien has a master's degree in business administration with an emphasis on American Indian Entrepreneurship. He is also an Apple certified trainer who is helping the college explore new ways to generate revenue. For example, visitors to the college Web site (www.menominee.edu) can download content from iTunes, and the college gets a share of the proceeds.

Sustainability Partners

The U.S. Department of Agriculture (USDA) is the largest supporter of the college's initiatives in developing academic programs and doing research and outreach, according to SDI Director Melissa Cook. In 2004, the Menominee Nation and the U.S. Forest Service (an agency of USDA) created the National Center for First Americans Forestlands at the college. It is designed to serve the Native stewards of forested lands throughout the country and internationally. In the United States, 44 American Indian tribes own more than 16 million acres of forestland. Mike Dockry has been the USDA Forest Service liaison to the college for four years. He served in the Peace Corps in Bolivia for three years and continues to do research there and to work closely with other international visitors to Menominee. In the future, his office plans to work with other tribal colleges and tribes across the country.

The Sustainable Development Institute holds an international conference every three years: "Sharing Indigenous Wisdom: An International Dialogue on Sustainable Development." The first in June 2004 was sponsored by the W. K. Kellogg Foundation, and the second in June 2007 was sponsored by the Ford Foundation, Menominee Tribal Enterprises, and the U.S. Forest Service. Another is planned in 2010.

Students are always involved in the international conferences; college administrators believe it is important to broaden their perspective. The experience instills tribal pride in students as well as humility about their own problems. Patrick Waukau, an intern at SDI, met people from all over the world who respected the Menominee sustainable forest model. "People from that far away actually knew who we were; people across the state don't know us," he said. He learned that many of the indigenous people elsewhere in the world are now fighting for their land and for their resource rights, struggles that the Menominee endured decades ago. In addition to the conferences, the college has frequent visits from indigenous people in other parts of the world.

The tribal college has participated in many national efforts related to sustainability that involve students. In February 2009, the SDI organized a National Teach-In on Climate Change. For the session on Philosophy and Spirituality, local priests, ministers, and Menominee elders discussed how spirituality, culture, and personal philosophy relate to sustainability.

CMN has a chapter of SEEDS (Strategies for Ecology Education Development and Sustainability), which is an education program of the Ecological Society of America. About 11 tribal colleges have chapters. For one project, the students who traveled to Chiapas started a campus coffeehouse that serves fair trade, organic, shade-grown, and bird-friendly coffee they selected from the coffee cooperative in Mexico.

Some of the other national programs related to sustainability that the college has participated in are:

- the National Wildlife Federation's National Chill Out (http://www.nwf. org/campusEcology/chillout/) competition;
- Recyclemania (http://www.recyclemaniacs.org), a nationwide college contest to reduce the waste produced on campus by recycling papers, plastics, and aluminum;
- Native American Fish and Wildlife Society conferences; and
- Campus Climate Challenge, a project of Energy Action Coalition, which asks college youth to promote, organize, and initiate a clean energy future.

CHALLENGES

All tribal colleges and universities are chronically underfunded and the staff overextended. They serve students with tremendous needs and are chartered by tribes that have limited resources. Most TCUs struggle to find enough faculty members with advanced degrees who are willing to work in isolated rural communities. While the Menominee college faces these challenges, it has found some ways to address them.

CMN President Fowler encourages her deans to get advanced degrees and offers incentives and support for them to do so. Located only 40 miles from Green Bay, WI, and also near the Oneida Reservation, the college is not as isolated as many. The Oneida Tribe provides generous scholarships to all eligible tribal members, many of whom get advanced degrees and want to come home, but the Oneida Tribe cannot employ all of them and has no tribal college of its own. Fowler said she likes having non-Indian faculty and faculty from other tribes, who bring their own talents and knowledge to the college.

While the college and its Sustainable Development Institute complement one another, SDI requires additional staff and funding for research and outreach, beyond that required for the college's teaching mission. The college's partnerships with national organizations—especially the U.S. Forest Service—are crucial to SDI's viability.

The college staff and faculty say Fowler is an incredible networker, and the college has several very good grant writers. Fowler travels on average two weeks out of every month. She serves on boards of many organizations relevant to her college's interests, especially organizations that will pay her travel expenses.

Fowler emphasizes the importance of grant management and accountability. She has an office of sponsored programs to direct grants administration. She has an annual audit, and for the last 10-12 years, the auditors have found no problems. Auditors from the U.S. Inspector General's office recently spent two weeks at CMN looking into a federal grant, according to Fowler. When they left, one of the auditors told her he had no recommendations for improvement; he had never seen such good documentation.

The college and SDI depend heavily upon grants and have several good grant writers. In fact over half of the college's annual budget is derived from grants, according to Fowler. Many institutions find such dependence on grants frightening; staff positions are vulnerable. At SDI, the new, innovative initiatives in particular are funded by grants, according to the director, Melissa Cook. She points out that research and development require trial and error, and funding organizations needs to understand that.

One challenge faced by some other tribal colleges and universities does not seem to be a problem at Menominee. Tribal college faculty and administrators elsewhere sometimes agonize over theoretical interpretations of cultural principles. At College of Menominee Nation, however, the administrators and faculty seem to understand and agree that sustainability is the basis for the cultural mission of the college. While there could be disagreements about how broadly sustainability should be defined, the concept itself seems to be universally accepted.

Advice For Colleagues at Other Tribal Colleges and Universities

The student learning experience at the College of Menominee Nation depends heavily upon internships. If the students are selected carefully, they can expand the capability of the overextended staff. Precautions must be taken, however, said USDA Forest Service liaison Mike Dockry. "If you look at it as a learning experience for the students, then everything falls into line," he said. "If you approach it as just another person to work in the office, it does not work." The organization must have people who have time to work with the intern. The students must be people who are able to work independently. If they are not, they might be better for work/ study positions, making copies and other office tasks. At Menominee, applicants go through a rigorous job application process; they are told that their positions are important and prestigious. The interns should have some projects to work on independently and some to work on with other staff. Most are paid.

Melissa Cook recommends that other tribal colleges approach federal agencies about partnerships. The mission of the National Center for First Americans Forestlands at Menominee is to serve all the Native stewards of forested lands throughout the United States. However, Cook said this does not necessarily preclude partnerships between the U.S. Forest Service and other tribal colleges. The Forest Service has a lot of resources and expertise to share. The agency and the college have a reciprocal relationship: The agency is interested in the Menominee forests, which provide an area of research and comparison for them. Other tribal colleges might be able to create similar models using their grasslands or prairie lands, Cook said.

Many federal agencies are involved with natural resources, some of which already have relationships with tribal colleges, such as the Bureau of Land Management, the U.S. Fish and Wildlife Service, the U.S. Environmental Protection Agency, the U. S. Geological Survey, and other agencies of the U.S. Department of Agriculture (USDA). Since tribal colleges and universities are land grant colleges, they have a natural partnership with USDA, which can be further developed. College of Menominee has also worked closely with the National Science Foundation's All Nations Louis Stokes Alliance for Minority Participation and NASA.

President Fowler recommends that other tribal colleges consider participating in the Clinton Global Initiative and national climate change organizations. At national meetings and private meetings with Clinton, she has consistently emphasized the importance of including voices of other Native people. The College of Menominee Nation has received some financial support from the Clinton Initiative for its sustainability work. In addition, the other participants presumably have benefited from the wisdom of the Menominee.

CONCLUSION

At national meetings where Fowler has spoken, participants expressed surprise that her college requires all students to take the Introduction to Sustainability course. Fowler pointed out that TCUs have flexibility that long-established institutions don't have. A tribal college can respond more quickly than a larger, older university to changing technologies and societal situations. Talks with faculty, staff, and interns at CMN indicated that they feel their suggestions and ideas are valued, which means that the staff and faculty are energized for their work.

A tribal college can be energized by spirituality as well. As part of the National Teach-In on Global Warming, the college included a session on philosophy and spirituality, a topic rarely broached anywhere else. Melissa Cook said, "Spirituality is one of the core concepts of sustainability—the connection you have with yourself, with the world, with the institution you work for. Without that connection, you don't find the meanings behind your actions, the relevance. It is the base of all relationships."

For too long, money has replaced spirituality for meaning, she said. "People are trying to go back to what has been meaningful. A lot of people are looking to tribal people for our experiences and our knowledge. Tribes have the wisdom to continue being. That is what sustainability is all about—helping others because what other people do to the earth will affect us, too."

Marjane Ambler is former editor of *Tribal College: Journal of American Indian Higher Education*. She writes frequently about issues in Indian Country and is the author of *Breaking the Iron Bonds: Indian Control of Energy Development*, published by the University of Kansas Press.

Further Reading

The *Tribal College Journal* has published three issues devoted to sustainability, and each had a resource guide with annotated references to relevant books, articles, organizations, and websites. All three Resource Guides are available online at www.tribalcollegejournal.org :

Vol. 13, No. 3 (spring 2002). This issue focuses on the importance of sustainable social and economic institutions.

Vol. 17, No. 2 (winter 2005). This issue focuses on alternative energy and conservation. It includes an article about a cultural exchange between the Mayan people of Belize and the Menominee and a profile of Chris Caldwell, a graduate of CMN and the University of Wisconsin - Madison, and his vision for the sustainability of the Menominee forest.

Vol. 20, No. 2 (winter 2008). This issue focused on four tribal colleges, including the Menominee, and their efforts to go green.

Davis, Thomas. *Sustaining the Forest, the People, and the Spirit.* Albany: State University of New York Press, 2000.

Davis, who has been involved in the tribal college movement from its beginnings, worked at the College of Menominee Nation for many years. In this book, he explores the Menominee Tribe's conception of sustainable development and its cultural commitment to sustained-yield forest management.

Web sites for national programs that the College of Menominee Nation is involved with:

Clinton Global Initiative: http://www.clintonglobalinitiative.org/

US Environmental Protection Agency's Energy Star (www.energystar.gov)

American College and University Presidents' Climate Commitment http://www.presidentsclimatecommitment.org/

Campus Climate Challenge, a project of Energy Action Coalition, which asks college youth to promote, organize, and initiate a clean energy future.: http://climatechallenge.org

SEEDS (Strategies for Ecology Education Development and Sustainability), which is an education program of the Ecological Society of America. http://www.esa.org/seeds/

The National Wildlife Federation's National Chill Out (http://www.nwf.org/campusEcology/chillout/)

Recyclemania (http://www.recyclemaniacs.org), a nationwide college contest to reduce the waste produced on campus by recycling papers, plastics, and aluminum.

Native American Fish and Wildlife Society http://www.nafws.org/

National Teach-in on global Warming: http://www.nationalteachin.org/index.php

College of Menominee Nation and Sustainable Development Institute web sites:

www.menominee.edu

http://www.sustainabledevelopmentinstitute.org

2nd international conference: http://sharingindigenouswisdom.org/conference/sharing_indigenous_wisdom_conference.asp

The Computer Engineering Degree Program at Salish Kootenai College

Timothy Olson

Salish Kootenai College recently established a baccalaureate degree program in computer engineering and graduated the first students from this program in 2009. The computer engineering degree program is built upon experience in providing a two-year engineering transfer preparation program since 1996. The development of pedagogical approaches that teach computer engineering through substantial use of traditional tribal cultural approaches has been challenging, but study of current and future economic development issues on Indian reservations and constructive roles the engineering profession can play are prominent in the computer engineering degree program. Engineering education at Salish Kootenai College supports the long-term economic development of the Flathead Indian Reservation and tribal economic and governmental sovereignty, and hence indirectly supports the preservation of the cultures of the Salish, Pend d'Oreille, and Kootenai peoples. The computer engineering program is accredited by the Northwest Commission on Colleges and Universities. Salish Kootenai College is working toward accreditation by ABET, the national engineering accrediting organization.

The Flathead Reservation and SKC Context

Salish Kootenai College is located on the 1.3 million-acre Flathead Indian Reservation in western Montana, the home of the Confederated Salish and Kootenai Tribes. For countless generations the Salish, Pend d'Oreille, and Kootenai people occupied a much larger aboriginal territory of tens of millions of acres in present day Montana, Idaho, Washington, Wyoming, and Canada. The

Salish and Pend d'Oreille people were once part of a single, large Salish-speaking tribal nation that lived in the Pacific northwest region that later reorganized into smaller tribes. The Kootenai people of the Flathead Reservation are members of the Ksanka band of the Ktunaxa Nation. Canada is the home of five other bands of the Ktunaxa Nation, and an additional band resides in Idaho. Kootenai language and culture is distinct from the language and culture of the Salish and Pend d'Oreille people.

By the mid 1800's the encroachment of other tribes into the aboriginal territory of the Salish, Pend d'Oreille, and Kootenai people, caused by westward settler movements and U.S. government policies, adversely impacted the economies of the tribes and led to more intense conflicts with other tribes. Epidemic disease that accompanied traders and trappers utilizing the tribes' aboriginal territory led to high mortality, especially among children and elders. Due to these pressures, the leaders of the Salish, Pend d'Oreille, and Kootenai people agreed to a treaty with the U.S. government that established the Flathead Indian Reservation with its current boundaries. In 1910 the U.S. government opened the Flathead Reservation to non-Indian homesteaders over the objections of the Confederated Salish and Kootenai Tribes. This action led to the ownership of over 60 percent of the area within the reservation boundaries by non-Indians by the time the Confederated Salish and Kootenai Tribes adopted a tribal constitution and a council form of government under the federal Indian Reorganization Act of 1934. Since that time the tribes have implemented a land acquisition policy that has increased the area of land within the reservation under tribal or individual tribal member ownership to 63 percent. The current reservation population is approximately 25,000, with about 11,000 people of Indian descent. About 4,200 of these 11,000 people of Indian descent are members of the Confederated Salish and Kootenai Tribes. The other residents of Indian descent are either members of other tribal nations, descendents of members of the Confederated Salish and Kootenai Tribes who are ineligible for tribal enrollment, or descendents of other tribes.

Salish Kootenai College was chartered in 1977 by the Confederated Salish and Kootenai Tribes with the goal of increasing the number of tribal members that complete post-secondary education programs. SKC was first accredited as a two-year college in 1984 by the Northwest Commission of Colleges and Universities, and as a four-year college in 1998. The mission of SKC is "to provide quality postsecondary educational opportunities for Native Americans locally and from throughout the United States." It is also part of the college mission to "assist with the preservation of the cultures, languages, histories, and natural environment of the Salish, Pend d'Oreille, and Kootenai people," and to "assist the Indian community with the economic development needs of the Flathead Indian Nation." While the college encourages diversity in its student population, its primary purpose is to serve the needs of Native American people. Student enrollment was 1,040 in the 2007-08 academic year, and 21 percent were declared majors in one of the ten SKC STEM degree programs. Native American students (meaning students enrolled in a federally recognized tribe, or students who are first or second generation descendents of a member of a federally recognized tribe) were 74 percent of this enrollment and represented 55 different tribes.

THE MOTIVATION FOR ENGINEERING EDUCATION AT SALISH KOOTENAI COLLEGE

Salish Kootenai College offers five one-year certificates, thirteen associate degrees, and nine bachelor degrees, many of which are professionally oriented. The offering of these degree programs is a substantial part of the college mission as providing these educational opportunities assists individual students seeking to improve their earning capacity in order to support themselves and their families. Collectively these graduates help maintain and grow the economy of the Flathead Reservation, and so help maintain the vitality of the Confederated Salish and Kootenai Tribes and cultures of the tribes.

Baccalaureate degree programs offered by Salish Kootenai College:

Business	Forestry
Computer Engineering	Information Technology
Early Childhood Education	Nursing
Elementary Education	Social Work
Environmental Science	

The Confederated Salish and Kootenai Tribes have exerted their sovereign rights to deliver and manage many important infrastructure, government, and business functions on the Flathead Reservation ("Confederated Salish & Kootenai Tribes"). This management includes Mission Valley Power (the local electric utility) and joint operation of a large hydroelectric facility (Kerr Dam), tribal housing, tribal health services, the safety of dams program, tribal lands including substantial forest resources, tourism and recreation, and fish and wildlife resources. The tribes also own and operate several technology and engineering services firms that do business across the United States. These businesses include S&K Aerospace, S&K Global Solutions, S&K Technologies, and S&K Electronics ("CSKT—Tribal Affiliated Businesses").

The engineering education programs offered by Salish Kootenai College will provide future employees for these businesses, and later in their careers these graduates are expected to play prominent roles in starting new businesses.

The Engineering Transfer Preparation Program

In 1993 Salish Kootenai College began the expansion of its A.S. in Environmental Science degree into a four-year program. The author was hired in 1995 to support this new B.S. degree program through developing and teaching a two-quarter algebra-based physics sequence and teaching existing classes in pre-calculus and calculus. In 1996 the author recommended that the college create a two-year transfer preparation program in engineering, and President Dr. Joseph McDonald and then Academic Vice President Gerald Slater directed the author to develop this program. From 1996 to 2000 several new classes were created: a three-quarter calculus-based physics sequence, two new calculus classes that expanded the single existing one-quarter calculus class into a complete year-long sequence, two additional mathematics classes on differential equations and multivariable calculus, and five engineering classes (engineering statics, engineering dynamics, mechanics of materials, thermodynamics, and fluid mechanics). These new classes supported students interested in transferring to another university to complete a baccalaureate degree in civil, mechanical, or environmental engineering or a related engineering specialty. Classes in electrical engineering laboratory techniques and electric circuit analysis were created in 2003 for students interested in transferring for B.S. degrees in electrical or computer engineering.

The college's engineering transfer preparation program had modest success during the period from 1996 up to opening of the computer engineering B.S. degree program in 2007. An average of two to three students a year began their engineering education at SKC and either successfully found employment on the Flathead Reservation after completing the transfer preparation program, or transferred into an engineering degree program elsewhere, most commonly within Montana at Montana State University in Bozeman. Other transfer institutions have included Montana Tech of the University of Montana, the University of Idaho, and Northern Arizona University. The success of these students upon transfer has not been rigorously tracked, but partial evidence suggests the baccalaureate degree completion rate has been relatively low at approximately one third. Some of these students have had significant success. For example, an electrical engineering student completed both B.S. and M.S. degrees in electrical engineering. A mechanical engineering student returned to the Flathead Reservation after earning the B.S. degree to work for S&K Electronics, and then as an engineer for a local lumber business. A civil engineering student now works for the federal Bureau of Land Management.

An important motivating factor for the creation of the computer engineering baccalaureate program was the desire to increase the number of students who declare a major in engineering. Another important factor was a goal of significantly increasing the percentage of engineering majors that complete the degree above the approximately one third that had completed the degree at a transfer institution. An increase in the degree completion rate has occurred when several other professional B.A. and B.S. programs were created by SKC, notably in nursing, social work, elementary education, information technology, environmental science, and forestry. Before Salish Kootenai College offered four-year degrees in these areas few students starting their education at SKC successfully completed a four-year program in one of these six majors at a transfer institution. In the 2008-09 academic year there were 80 total majors in these six baccalaureate degree programs, with 28 graduates. The hypothesis is that a similar result can be expected for engineering: more students will declare an engineering major and complete the degree if they are able to fully pursue their educational goals in a more familiar tribal-oriented educational setting.

THE DEVELOPMENT OF THE B.S. IN COMPUTER ENGINEERING DEGREE PROGRAM

Salish Kootenai College began studying the desirability and feasibility of developing a baccalaureate engineering degree in 2003. Many people contributed to the decision making process. Two engineers from NASA Johnson Space Center (Lee Snapp, since retired from NASA, and Scott Askew) were stationed for a year each at SKC under the NASA Administrator's Fellowship program ("NASA Administrator's Fellowship Program") and assisted the author with consideration of various engineering specialty degree options and the development of some engineering classes. Senior management from S&K Electronics and S&K Technologies, two local tribal technology businesses, provided advice on the need for engineering graduates for their businesses and tribal agencies. Several SKC faculty members experienced in developing and teaching STEM degree programs, especially Department of Natural Resources Chairman Bill Swaney, assisted in the analyses.

Three options emerged from these analyses. One was to not develop a four-year engineering degree program and focus instead on continued support and improvement of the existing engineering transfer preparation program. The second option was to develop a civil engineering B.S. degree program. The argument for this choice centered on meeting the need for engineers with strong ties to the local community who could maintain and develop civil infrastructure (roads, bridges, housing, water systems, power systems, etc.) on the Flathead Reservation and other Indian reservations throughout the U.S. The availability of community members with the education to assume engineering and engineering management roles would aid tribal communities wishing to exert greater sovereignty over their civil infrastructure. Arguing against this option was the need for substantial facility and laboratory upgrades; more than $1 million would be required to house and equip a civil engineering program that would meet accreditation standards. There were also concerns about the limited opportunities for additional job growth in civil engineering on the Flathead Reservation and other tribal communities once the immediate employment needs were met.

The third option was to develop a computer engineering B.S. degree program. The argument for this option was the relatively low facility and laboratory costs (in comparison to civil engineering), and the desire for long-term, environmentally benign economic opportunities for the Flathead Reservation and other tribal communities that would lead to employment not only for engineering graduates, but also for tribal members in non-engineering support positions. Computer engineering offers more of an opportunity for growth in employment on the Flathead Reservation than civil engineering. The main drawback of this option is that it does not fully address the need for civil engineers and greater tribal sovereignty over tribal civil infrastructure.

Two key events helped trigger the final decision to proceed with the new computer engineering degree program. From 2002-2007 Salish Kootenai College developed, with financial support from the National Science Foundation's Tribal Colleges and Universities Program ("NSF TCUP"), a B.S. degree program in information technology built upon its existing A.S. degree program in information technology. The successful development of the B.S. in information technology degree program provided the college with valuable experience in creating a baccalaureate program in an area related to engineering, and provided evidence to funding agencies that SKC was capable of developing a four-year engineering program. The significant increase in information technology majors from around 20 to near 60 provided evidence that there would be a substantial increase in engineering majors should the college offer a four-year engineering degree program.

Another key event was the offer in 2004 from the then-Deputy Director of the Applied Engineering and Technology Directorate at NASA Goddard Space Flight Center, Bruce Butterworth, to provide the center's assistance if the college were to decide to develop a four-year engineering degree. This assistance would include providing guidance on degree program development, and assistance of Goddard Space Flight Center engineers as adjunct faculty during the development phase. The author met Mr. Butterworth at the May 2004 Tribal College and University Conference hosted by the NASA Jet Propulsion Laboratory and organized by Mary Anne Stoutsenberger from the NASA Tribal Colleges and Universities Program and Carrie Billy from the American Indian Higher Education Consortium. SKC accepted the offer of assistance in summer 2005, and President McDonald decided to recommend the development of a B.S. in computer engineering program to the SKC Board Directors in fall 2005.

SKC proceeded with the development of the B.S. in computer engineering program in earnest in the 2005-06 academic year. Goddard engineers helped form an external advisory committee consisting of people familiar with tribal technology businesses, engineering education, and ABET accreditation processes. To date the advisory committee has met twice at SKC (October 2005 and June 2007) and once by telecon (June 2006). The advisory committee assisted in the development of program educational objectives and the degree plan, and with preparation for the ABET accreditation process. The degree plan in place today is based upon a combination of advisory committee recommendations, computer engineering professional society recommendations ("Computer Engineering 2004"), and SKC faculty experience with STEM degree programs, especially experience gained from its engineering transfer preparation and B.S. in information technology programs. The degree plan was approved by the SKC faculty Curriculum Committee and the board of directors in winter 2006.

Salish Kootenai College computer engineering external advisory committee members:

Larry Hall, General Manager, S&K Electronics

Dr. Michael Leonard, Senior Associate Dean of Engineering, Mercer University

Dr. Jerome Saltzer, Professor of Computer Science and Engineering, Massachusetts Institute of Technology

Bruce Butterworth, Deputy Director, Applied Engineering and Technology Directorate, NASA Goddard Space Flight Center

Dr. Bruce Kramer, Senior Advisor for Engineering, National Science Foundation

Dr. Robert Marley, Dean of Engineering, Montana State University

Steve Clairmont, Manager, S&K Technologies

Dr. Norman Fortenberry, Director of the Center for the Advancement of Scholarship on Engineering Education, National Academy of Engineering

The next step was to seek permission from the Northwest Commission of Colleges and Universities (NWCCU) to open the B.S in computer engineering program for student admissions fall quarter 2006. The request was prepared and submitted in spring 2006. The request included assurances that the college would be able to acquire the needed financial resources to develop and maintain the degree program from fall 2006 through spring 2010 by a combination of tuition, Tribal College Act federal funding, and grant funding expected from pending grants. NWCCU deferred making an accreditation decision until the college was successful with the pending grant requests. This delayed the opening of the degree program to fall 2007. In the meantime SKC continued with program development and experimental offerings of some of the classes in the new degree plan. SKC was able to report success to NWCCU with the grant applications in January 2007, and NWCCU accredited the B.S. in computer engineering degree program in June 2007. The new degree program was officially opened for student admissions in fall 2007.

NASA Goddard Space Flight Center assistance was also important in developing and offering several of the new computer engineering classes. One Goddard engineer worked as an adjunct faculty member each academic quarter, developing and teaching one of the new classes from the degree program each quarter from winter quarter 2006 though spring quarter 2008. Typically the adjunct instructor would be in residence at the college for two weeks during the ten-week quarter, and teach the remainder of the class from Maryland using Internet videoconferencing technology. In addition, one engineer, Dr. Tracee Jamison, worked full time in the computer engineering program in residence at the college in the 2008–09 academic year through the NASA Administrator's Fellowship Program.

The first student graduated from the computer engineering program in June 2009. Two more graduates are expected after fall quarter 2010. Even though the degree program did not open for student admissions until fall 2007 these students were already taking classes in anticipation of the coming new degree program while the program was under development and classes were first offered on an experimental basis. In spring quarter 2009 there were thirteen declared computer engineering majors.

FUTURE PLANS

ABET accreditation is the remaining major task in the development of Salish Kootenai College's computer engineering B.S. program. ABET, Inc. is a federation of 30 professional and technical societies that accredits college and university applied science, computing, engineering, and technology programs in the

United States. ABET accreditation of the college's program is desirable for several reasons. ABET accreditation assures potential employers of graduates that the academic program meets national-level quality standards. Graduation from an ABET-accredited program is a requirement for employment eligibility for many federal and private sector engineering jobs, and is sometimes required for eligibility for enrollment in graduate-level engineering degree programs.

A college or university must successfully complete several steps before ABET will grant a new degree program initial accreditation ("Information for Programs Seeking Initial Accreditation"). These steps include the development of program educational objectives, development and offering of the degree plan based upon the program educational objectives, implementation of a comprehensive plan of assessment and analysis of program effectiveness, and preparation of a program self-study ("Criteria for Accrediting Engineering Programs"). An institution seeking initial program accreditation is eligible for the initial ABET accreditation site visit after the completion of the self-study and the graduation of the first student. SKC is anticipating the completion of the self-study by summer 2010, and the ABET site visit in fall 2010.

Although the computer engineering B.S. program is now the primary focus for engineering education at SKC, plans are to continue offering the option for engineering transfer preparation for students interested in other engineering specialties. A lower demand for transfer preparation is anticipated because of the existence of the computer engineering four-year degree. SKC has no plans to create any additional baccalaureate degrees in another engineering specialty within the next ten years.

LESSONS LEARNED

Several key lessons learned can be identified in reviewing the history of the development of engineering education at SKC. These observations may be of significance to other tribal colleges considering developing their own two- or four-year engineering technology programs or four-year engineering programs.

Careful consideration should be given to whether or not the development of engineering or engineering technology programs are sensible for the institution and the local community. Are more students graduating with engineering technology or engineering degrees needed to achieve the sovereignty and economic development goals of the local community? Does the institution have or can it acquire the human and financial resources needed to develop and deliver the program? Would a focus on engineering technology programs, or engineering transfer preparation be more feasible and still meet local sovereignty and economic development goals? In the case of the Flathead Reservation and SKC, extensive effort had been devoted to an engineering transfer preparation program for over ten years with some success. However, the production of engineering graduates who started at SKC and completed the four-degree at a transfer institution has resisted growth beyond one or two students a year. It is clear more engineering graduates are needed in order to meet the community goal of exerting greater sovereignty over infrastructure on the Flathead Reservation, and in order to promote the long-term economic prospects for the Confederated Salish and Kootenai Tribes and individual tribal members and their families. Hence offering baccalaureate-level engineering education makes sense in the Flathead Reservation and SKC context.

For Salish Kootenai College long-term partnerships with regional universities and with federal agencies was critical. It is unlikely the college would have been able to develop a four-year engineering degree program for several years yet without this assistance. The partnerships that had the biggest impact were at least five years in duration.

Recruitment of qualified faculty for the computer engineering degree program has proven to be more challenging than was anticipated in the planning phase. SKC does not follow the tenure system, and that proved to be a major impediment for several potential engineering faculty candidates recruited by national searches. Ultimately it was personal contacts developed through the partnership with NASA Goddard Space Flight Center, rather than local and national advertising of faculty openings, that led to successful recruitment.

It is important to have entry and exit points between engineering and related degree programs. SKC offers A.S. and B.S. in degrees in information technology and an A.S. in engineering graphics. To date about half of the students entering the computer engineering program changed majors from information technology. Typically these students were successful in the I.T. program but desired more of a challenge. Apparently they did not have the confidence to start first in the engineering program, or didn't know enough about engineering to consider that option when first entering college. There is some overlap between I.T. and computer engineering degree requirements, such as programming, that enable students to move between the degree programs without starting completely over. Students that aren't successful in the computer engineering program or who decide engineering isn't the right career choice for them have the option of moving into the I.T. or engineering graphics programs without having to start completely over.

Salish Kootenai College embraces the use of tribal cultural knowledge and values in designing degree programs that teach through this culture and these values. Several STEM degree programs at the college use this pedagogical approach extensively, notable the forestry and environmental science programs. Incorporating culturally oriented pedagogy has been challenging for the SKC computer engineering program as computer technology was not integrated into tribal life as was, for example, knowledge and use of the forests and fish and wildlife resources. One way where both traditional tribal scholarship and "Western" engineering approaches reinforce each other is using team-oriented approaches to develop solutions that help solve societal problems. Many SKC engineering students are strongly oriented to work in teams towards finding solutions that help their tribal communities and society at large. Engineers with strong team member and team leader skills are highly valued in the work force. Hence the SKC computer engineering program places a strong emphasis on team-oriented engineering design.

References

"Criteria for Accrediting Engineering Programs." ABET. 1 December 2008. ABET Engineering Accreditation Commission. 23 March 2009 <http://abet.org/forms.shtml>.

"Confederated Salish & Kootenai Tribes". CSKT. 23 March 2009 <www.cskt.org>

"CSKT—Tribal Affiliated Businesses." CSKT—Tribal Affiliated Businesses. 23 March 2009 <http://www.cskt.org/about/affiliated.htm>.

"Computer Engineering 2004: Curriculum Guidelines for Undergraduate Degree Programs in Computer Engineering." Curriculum Recommendations—Association for Computing Machinery. 12 December 2004. The Joint Task Force on omputing Curricula, IEEE Computer Society and Association for Computing Machinery. 23 March 2009 < http://www.acm.org/education/curricula-recommendations>.

"Information for Programs Seeking Initial Accreditation." ABET. 1 October 2008. ABET, Inc. 23 March 2009 <http://abet.org/new_programs.shtml>.

"NASA Administrator's Fellowship Program." UNCFSP—Science & Technology—NAFP—About. 23 March 2009 <http://www.uncfsp.org/spknowledge/default.aspx?page=program.view&areaid=1&contentid=179&typeid=nafp>.

"NSF TCUP". nsf.gov—Funding—Tribal Colleges and Universities Program—US National Science Foundation (NSF). 23 March 2009 <http://www.nsf.gov/funding/pgm_summ.jsp?pims_id=5483>.

Timothy Olson has worked at Salish Kootenai College since 1995 as a faculty member and administrator. In addition to leading the development and offering of SKC engineering education programs he serves as Chairman of the SKC Division of Sciences. He holds bachelor's and master's degrees in physics from the University of Minnesota, and a Ph. D. in physics from Montana State University.

Internet to the Hogan: A Wireless Weaving

Tom Davis

The Navajo Nation, located in three states, New Mexico, Arizona, and Utah, is the size of West Virginia. High mountain peaks, mesas, high desert, spectacular rock formations, volcanic fields, and canyon lands combine with generational poverty and scattered, remote communities located down miles of dirt roads to make Navajo the heart of the digital divide in the United States.

Definition of the Digital Divide

According to a report released by the Department of Commerce in 1995, "the 'digital divide'—the divide between those with access to new technologies and those without—is now one of America's leading economic and civil rights issues."[1] According to the report's Introduction by William M. Daly, then Secretary of Commerce,

> Ensuring access to the fundamental tools of the digital economy is one of the most significant investments our nation can make. Our country's most important resource is its people. Our companies are only as good as their workers. Highly-skilled, well educated workers make for stellar businesses and create superior products. In a society that increasingly relies on computers and the Internet to deliver information and enhance communication, we need to make sure that all Americans have access. Our domestic and global economies will demand it. Ready access to telecommunications tools will help produce the kind of technology-literate work force that will enable the United States to continue to be a leader in the global economy.[2]

The digital divide's consequences range far beyond economics, however. Technological developments have improved communication, health care, public services, public safety, entertainment, education, and even the ability to engage in creative endeavors for millions of people. By missing out on opportunities new technologies represent, the Navajo people are limited in their ability to fully participate in the contemporary world.

The Internet to the Hogan

The Internet to the Hogan Project (ITTH) at Navajo Technical College has been developed in order to provide a model for ending the digital divide in the Navajo Nation. Multi-faceted, the project has human, economic, educational, medical, public safety, research, and cultural aspects. It is designed to deploy cutting edge technologies in communities that in the past have acquired those technologies only after they have become commodities. What those who have developed the project are hoping is that the technologies put into place will address a range of issues that have kept the Navajo Nation from progressing economically since the European invasion of Navajo territory in the eighteenth century.

Leonard Tsosie, who was then a New Mexico state senator, named the project "Internet to the Hogan." A Hogan is a Navajo's home, he said, the place of family and the heart of culture. The Internet represents the contemporary world of technology. The Internet to the Hogan Project connects the contemporary world and the traditional Navajo home. Navajos can use that connection to improve their position in economic society while still participating in their rich family, clan, and cultural traditions. Carrie Billy (Navajo), Executive Director of the American Indian Higher Education Consortium (AIHEC), called the Internet to the Hogan Project an electronic weave. Navajo are famous for weaving rugs designed to reflect Navajo culture and the natural environment, she said. Weavers of the Internet to the Hogan Project are building an electronic weave that has the potential to benefit the Navajo Nation in the same way the Tennessee Valley Authority brought economic development to Appalachia after the Great Depression.

To express how culture and the Internet are interlinked in the Internet to the Hogan Project, Jared Ribble, one of the chief engineers of the project at Navajo Technical College, created a project logo encompassing a traditional Navajo basket, the idea of a radio dish used to broadcast high speed radio signals, and radio waves emanating from the dish:

"The Navajo believe deeply in four "R"s," according to Ribble in a 2009 conversation wtih the author: "Reverence, responsibility, relationships and respect. The Internet allows communication and relationships to be realized over distance. We want that communication and those relationships to be conducted

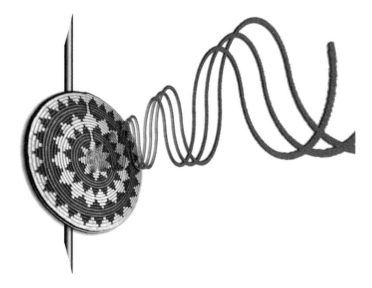

in the modern world using traditional concepts of reverence, responsibility, and respect. By emanating from the traditional basket, Internet to the Hogan brings the traditional and modern worlds together."

The Internet to the Hogan project has four major activities: Education of Navajo Tech staff and students in advanced wireless and high performance computing, partnership building within the United States' computational science community, deployment of an advanced OC3 (155 megabit) wireless network that can serve the Navajo Nation's most remote communities, and the Dinè Grid, which is designed to provide high value educational, telemedicine, public safety, research, and communication tools to the college and Navajo people.

Getting Internet to the Hogan Started

The Internet to the Hogan project started when James Tutt, then president of the Crownpoint Institute of Technology (the college's name before it became Navajo Technical College), decided to provide distance education to chapterhouses throughout the Navajo Nation. He asked for a plan that would solve technical and physical barriers to that goal.

The American Indian Higher Education Consortium's Technology Committee had partnered with an NSF funded project headquartered in Washington, D.C. called Advanced Networking for Minority Serving Institutions (ANMSI) to experiment with using microwave radio technology to provide Internet connectivity to Sitting Bull College and Turtle Mountain Community College in

2001–2002.[3] Experience gained from this work led to a grant proposal submitted to the Department of Defense that requested funding for a wireless network that would serve chapterhouses (community/government centers for Navajo communities) surrounding the college's Crownpoint, New Mexico campus.[4] The idea was to use this network to provide E-learning classes to chapterhouses and individual homes (hogans) with computers.

Shortly after the DOD proposal was funded, a New Mexico state senator, Leonard Tsosie, visited campus and was briefed on the proposed project. He became excited and convinced the legislature to fund the project's initial phase with $1.5 million grant. Jody Chase of NSF then allowed modifications to the college's existing Tribal College and Universities Project (TCUP) to provide additional support, and Internet to the Hogan was underway.

THE ENGINEERING DESIGNS

While project funding was being put together, several activities were undertaken simultaneously. The most important was to enroll IT staff in advanced degree programs. The IT director, Jason Arviso, had a baccalaureate degree and experience at Lucent Technologies, but other staff had Navajo Tech associate degrees. A partnership with Salish Kootenai College was developed so that Jared Ribble, who would become project engineer, and Chris Yazzie could begin baccalaureate degrees in information technology. Arviso enrolled in a Capella University master's degree program, and IT faculty were convinced to not only teach classes, but to also structure in-class student activities around ITTH and become involved in helping with project activities related to their expertise. IT staff agreed to teach classes for certificate and associate degree IT programs as they kept campus technology working and began the effort to build Internet to the Hogan. The idea was to blur the difference between IT practice and teaching in order to provide experiences seldom available to students.

As efforts to build Navajo technological expertise started, project leaders began to build partnerships with some of the country's most accomplished computational scientists. From October 15–17, 2000 in Palo Alto, California, under the leadership of Carrie Billy, now AIHEC's executive director but then executive director of the White House Initiative on Tribal Colleges and Universities (WHITCU), tribal college presidents sponsored a conference called "The Circle of Prosperity."[5] This conference gave Internet to the Hogan leaders individual and university contacts within the U.S.'s computational science community. It also provided ideas about how to use wireless technologies and high performance computing to end the digital divide and provide an infrastructure that could lead to greater prosperity on the chronically poor Navajo Nation.

The first partnership was with Hans Wehrner-Braun of the University of California at San Diego. Wehrner-Braun built an NSF funded experimental wireless network called High Performance Wireless Research and Education Network (HPWren), which "functions as a collaborative cyberinfrastructure on research, education, and first responder activities." "The network includes backbone nodes at University of California at San Diego and San Diego State University campuses, and a number of "hard to reach" areas in remote environments."[6] During a visit to Wehrner-Braun at the San Diego Supercomputing Center, Wehrner-Braun, Ribble, and the author came up with Internet To The Hogan's original design.

This design called for building an HPWren-like network, partially based on a Wehrner Braun designed wireless network for California tribes called the Tribal Digital Network, that would originate from land-based dark fiber brought to Crownpoint from Interstate 40 and distributed to sixteen surrounding communities. The design called for construction of three towers, solar power (via the Tribal Digital Village model) to power radios, and the use of water towers near chapterhouses to site radios capable of providing high speed Internet service in a thirty mile radius of each chapterhouse (see next page).

This design had weaknesses. The main drawback was that by originating the wireless signal from Crownpoint and radiating it outward, the cost of even a DS3, with a data rate of 44.736 Mbit/s, purchased from commercial vendors was prohibitive and made the project unsustainable.

By the time Ribble, who had now been joined by a new NSF director, Todd Romero, and the rest of the Navajo Tech team discovered the design problems, Senator Tsosie had introduced legislation in the New Mexico State legislature. When funding came through a new, more feasible, but more complex design, was produced.

In developing this design a partnership was formed with the Albuquerque High Performance Computing Center and the University of New Mexico's Information Technology Services. Information Technology Services controls a gigapop in downtown Albuquerque, New Mexico. A gigapop is short for "gigabit Point of Presence," a physical point that aggregates line based connectivity from different sources and supports data transfer rates of at least 1 Gbps. One Albuquerque Gigapop's link was with the National Lambda Rail, an important component of the new design. The Lambda Rail is an optical infrastructure that ensures the United States' research community "control and flexibility in meeting the requirements of the most advanced network applications and providing the resources demanded by cutting-edge network research."[7]

Under the new design the college would use three different wireless technologies to build an infrastructure that could, with enough funding, serve the entire Navajo Nation, giving the Nation control over its own infrastructure. The first project phase would start in downtown Albuquerque at the Gigapop, use long-range Harris microwave radios to connect to Crownpoint through four towers, two located on the Zia Pueblo Nation through a partnership between the

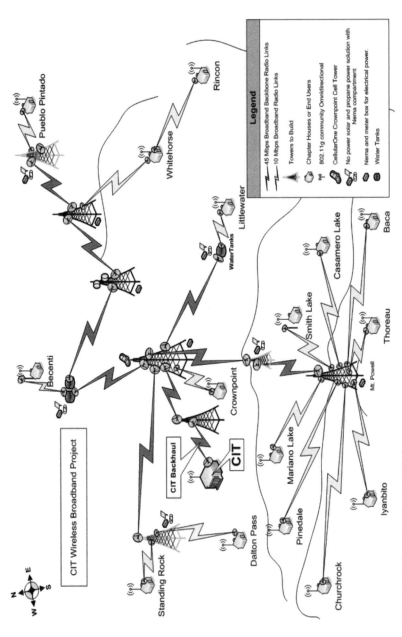

Illustration 1. Illustration by Jared Ribble

college and pueblo, one at a remote site called Chaco Ridge near Pueblo Pintado Chapterhouse, and the last built on a hill on Navajo Tech's Crownpoint campus. Radio signals would then be distributed using Motorola backhaul radios to chapterhouses surrounding Crownpoint. Motorola canopy technology, pioneered by Turtle Mountain Community College and ANMSI, would provide broadband connectivity to schools, hospital clinics, businesses, and homes in surrounding the chapterhouse.

Illustration 2 describes the path design of the new network; Illustration 3 (next page) shows the canopy design radiating from chapterhouses.

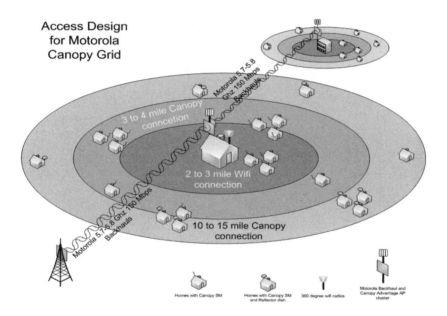

Illustration 2. Illustration by Jared Ribble

TeraGrid and the Cyberinfrastructure Design

As the effort was started to lease two towers at Zia Pueblo, a partnership was established with TeraGrid. Another NSF funded project, "TeraGrid is the world's largest, most comprehensive distributed cyberinfrastructure for open scientific research."

> Using high-performance network connections, the TeraGrid integrates high-performance computers, data resources and tools, and

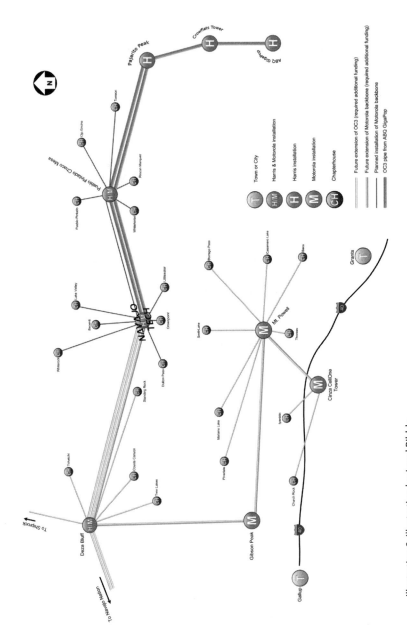

Illustration 3: Illustration by Jared Ribble

high-end experimental facilities around the country. Currently, TeraGrid resources include more than 750 teraflops of computing capability and more than 30 petabytes of online and archival data storage, with rapid access and retrieval over high-performance networks. Researchers can also access more than 100 discipline-specific databases.[8]

Work with the San Diego Supercomputing Center and Wehrner-Braun had shown how powerful a high performance network could be. It could not only deliver distance education to remote communities and provide an infrastructure for economic development, but it could also provide resources for telemedicine, public safety, and E-Government, along with other services useful to Navajo.

Scott Lathrop, education director for TeraGrid, worked with the Navajo Tech team, headed by Jason and Coleen Arviso, to bring a three day conference about high performance computing to the Navajo Tech campus. Tribal college instructors, teachers and students from Navajo schools, and Navajo Tech students were invited to attend. To date three education conferences have been held. The conferences are intended to educate the Navajo community about possible educational and cyberinfrastructure uses of Internet to the Hogan and the IBM Blade Center, which Ribble and his team had just installed on campus. Mark Trebian had also installed and started to teach the faculty about Moodle, an open source online teaching system, and was hoping to find tools that would build a sophisticated e-learning environment.[9]

One presentation during the first Navajo Tech conference featured computational scientists Tom Murphy and Charlie Peck. They had developed a small four bay multi-core computer, Little Fe, designed to help students learn about how high performance computers are constructed. In a brainstorming session on the conference's last day, the idea of the Dinè Grid was developed. The concept was that Navajo Tech students could be taught how to build Little Fe's so that they could be installed at schools and chapterhouses all over the Navajo Nation, creating a powerful distributed high performance computing grid at an exceptionally low cost.

THE DINÉ GRID

The Diné Grid architecture, arrived at during the brainstorming session, would be scalable in two ways. The most important of those had to do with usage. A user at a chapterhouse or home would be able to access the Internet at a minimal bandwidth, or they could access Supercomputing resources through the Albuquerque Gigapop to the TeraGrid. As Little Fe's were manufactured at Navajo Tech and

placed in chapterhouses, schools, public safety buildings, clinics, and other locations, the grid, tied together through software, would become increasingly powerful, adding resources to the whole system as new Little Fe's were brought online.
The distributed environment would also be scalable in that it would become increasingly powerful as a distributed high performance computer. The IBM Blade
Center on campus would be the center of the Dinè Grid. Every new Little Fe
would increase the supercomputing power available to users.[10]The power made
available through the grid would be linked into new tools developed by the high
performance computing community. Some of the new technologies envisioned
range from nano-technologies to data mining. In turn, these technologies would
improve reservation life in a wide range of areas, including education, telemedicine, public safety, e-government, economic development, remote sensing, and
research conducted by tribal government, Navajo Tech, Dinè College, and other
Navajo organizations.

Senator Tsosie's Partnership Building

As this design came into focus, Senator Tsosie started building a partnership with
a broad range of New Mexico and Navajo people and agencies. He started calling
monthly meetings to discuss topics such as how the Internet to the Hogan and
Diné Grid affected traditional Navajo culture, how the grid could bring advanced
telemedicine resources to remote Navajo communities, and how the grid could
lead to economic development. These meetings continued until Senator Tsosie
was elected a delegate to the Navajo Council and Linda Lovejoy, a member of the
college's board of trustees, replaced him in the state legislature. Important partnerships between Navajo Nation's Information Technology Department, particularly Harold Skow, the IT director, the University of New Mexico Hospital, and an
effort to work with Navajo elders to teach them about technology sponsored by
the New Mexico Library Association were built during this period. These partnerships continue to help define the work to create the Diné Grid.

Putting Internet to the Hogan and the
Diné Grid Together

The first effort to make wireless connectivity work on the Navajo Nation occurred
from an effort by Skow to provide telephone service to White Rock Chapterhouse
in Arizona. The chapter had never had a telephone, and Skow secured funding

from CISCO to install a wireless connection that could carry digital phone service. Skow, Navajo Tech, and CISCO technicians built the wireless connection as an Internet to the Hogan proof of concept.

After that project was completed, Navajo Tech upgraded wireless operations on campus, began securing a site for the Chaco Mesa tower, negotiated the Zia Pueblo partnership, installed T1 wireless connectivity for Zia, and secured a link to the Lambda Rail. As soon as this work was underway construction of the Navajo Tech campus tower started, followed by construction of the Chaco Mesa tower.

As soon as tower construction was completed, a solar panel array was built at the Chaco Mesa tower site to provide power. The Harris radios were installed at roughly the same time. As soon as the radios were installed benchmark testing started. Then backhaul Motorola radios were positioned and installed, followed by installation of canopy radios.

Currently the effort to put the Diné Grid in place is ongoing as is the effort to connect schools, medical clinics, and homes to ITTH. Diné Grid work is concentrating on building e-learning and telemedicine systems. The work on telemedicine is being done in partnership with the University of New Mexico hospital and Dr. Dale Alverso. The hope is that the e-learning system will be operational by 2010 with the telemedicine system to follow. Although additional funding will be needed to deploy Little Fe's, students at Navajo Tech are skilled at building them.

Economic development efforts, using the Internet to the Hogan effort as a showcase, are also underway. Al Kuslikis of the American Indian Higher Education Consortium is currently working with Navajo Tech in an effort to attract federal contractors in order to have them sub-contract with the college for Computer Aided Design and/or computational services. The college is in negotiation with Boeing, trying to work out an arrangement that will serve Boeing's needs while providing high skill/high wage jobs at Navajo Tech in Crownpoint.

The Hope and Dream of Internet to the Hogan and the Diné Grid

At the Prosperity Game in Palo Alto, California, the author gave a speech where he said that tribal people have always been passengers riding in the technology train's caboose rather than the train's engine as engineers. Unless the digital divide can be ended and tribal people can work their way up to the train's engine room where innovation results in the creation of new wealth, poverty is likely going to continue to plague Indian country.

By harnessing the power of the greatest technology engine in the world, the high performance computing community, Navajo Tech has embarked on an effort to change the dynamics of poverty on the Navajo Nation. This project is still in its infancy. A tremendous amount of work has been completed. This includes work associated with the Diné Grid, which is the most important part of the project since it provides abilities, tools, and knowledge to individual Navajo people. However, the project has yet to show concrete results.

Still, changes driven by the project have transformed the Navajo Tech campus. Not only does the campus operate with OC3 connectivity, solving frustrating connectivity and operational delays, but new courses and programs are also being generated at an increasing pace. The campus has developed an environment where success in all things technical is expected rather than hoped for, as was the case in the past. Most importantly of all, students are excited. Working on Internet to the Hogan or Diné Grid projects, they feel like they are not only mastering twenty-first century skills, but are also contributing to the Navajo Nation's future.

Navajo Culture and Internet to the Hogan

From a culture standpoint, technology presents several challenges. No Navajo words exist for computer, keyboard, Internet, server, or many other words associated with this initiative. Jeannie Whitehorse, a Navajo librarian who has worked with ITTH since Tsosie started forming local partnerships, has been working with tribal elders to teach about how technology can become part of Navajo cultural life. Whitehorse worked for months trying to explain basic technology concepts to elders without telephones, electricity, or running water, but they did not see the point until she used a paint program to show a group of traditional women how to use it to create rug designs. Then:

> I had these five grandmas all sitting around the notebook [computer], and they didn't want to go. The bus driver came to pick them up, and he was honking and honking. But the grandmas said, 'No, we want to finish our rug.' The bus driver gave up and came in and sat down and watched.[11]

Another effort the college has made to integrate culture into ITTH is to work with the Navajo film office to render in the IBM Blade Center videos and movies made about Navajo, including the rich treasure-house of films about Navajo culture.

At a deeper level the project has tried to use principles of the Diné Philosophy of Education to help continue successful deployment of technology resources for the Navajo people, interrupting the pattern where businesses develop the Nation's infrastructure and then abandon it when it becomes unprofitable, leaving Navajo without cable television, telephones, or other advances. The college's mission statement concludes with the following Navajo words: nitsáhákees, nahat'a, iiná, sihasin. These words contain a philosophy about how Navajos should go about *Nitsáhákees* (Thinking), *Nahat'á* (Planning), *Iiná* (Living) and *Sihasin* (Assuring). Internet to the Hogan and the Diné Grid have used this philosophy as guidance since its inception, always working toward a better future through education and technology for the Navajo people, thinking about what the project can accomplish, planning its deployment and the tools it can provide, trying to make it useful to the Navajo people, and examining its aspects in order to improve its operations over time.

ENDNOTES

1. National Telecommunications and Information Administration, United States Department of Commerce. 1995. *Falling Through the Net: Defining the Digital Divide.* Washington DC: Government Printing Office.
2. National Telecommunications and Information Administration, 1995, p. 1.
3. Both colleges are located in North Dakota.
4. Navajo Tech has campuses in Crownpoint, NM and Chinle, AZ.
5. Davis, Thomas and Trebian, Mark. January/February 2001. "Shaping the Destiny of Native American People by Ending the Digital Divide." *Educause Review*, Vol. 30, No. 1. Boulder, CO, p. 46. "The conference was modeled after Prosperity Games, a new type of forum for simulating and exploring complex issues in a variety of areas (economics, politics, environment, education, etc.) from a variety of perspectives, ranging from a global viewpoint down to the details of customer/supplier/market interactions in specific industries. Prosperity Games are an outgrowth of move/countermove and seminar war games that use game theory to develop the best strategies to cope with situations of conflict and cooperation. The concept was developed by J. Pace VanDevender and Marshall Berman from Sandia National Laboratories for a wide variety of applications."
6. High Performance Wireless and Research Network, http://hpwren.ucsd.edu. Accessed 11/11/2008,, pg. 1.
7. The National Lambda Rail, website. http://www.nlr.net/about. Accessed 11/11/2008.
8. TeraGrid. http://www.teragrid.org/about. Accessed 11/11/2008.
9. Later on Trebian and Jason Arviso began work with Stanford University and UC San Diego's High Performance Computing Center and Diane Baxter to integrate science gateways into the E-Learning design. A science gateway uses a combination of desktop computing, high performance computing, and the Internet to allow users to access information and tools useful to researchers in a range of disciplines, including astronomy, biology, chemistry, computer science, earth science, engineering, materials science, and physics. Working with the developers of the Geon Gateway, http://www.geongrid.org, which provides data, tools, webservices, and knowledge representation for exploring the geosciences, Trebian and Arviso are attempting to make the gateway useful to teachers and students at the middl, high school, and undergraduate levels of education.

10. Davis, Tom; Arviso, Jason; Ribble, Jared; Yazzie, Chris; and Trebian, Mark. June 2008. "Presentation to the Annual Meeting of the Navajo Technical College's Board of Trustees." Albuquerque, NM.
11. Pyrillis, Rita. May 2007. Fed Tech Magazine. "IT Across the Navajo Nation." Accessed from http://fedtechmagazine.com/article.asp?item_id+277, 11/27/2008.

Tom Davis is Dean of Instruction at Navajo Technical College in Crownpoint, New Mexico.